Liar, Liar

BY LAURENCE YEP

Sweetwater
Dragonwings
Child of the Owl
Sea Glass
Sea Demons
The Mark Twain Murders
Kind Hearts and Gentle Monsters
Dragon of the Lost Sea

Liar, Liar

LAURENCE YEP

William Morrow and Company
New York 1983

Copyright © 1983 by Laurence Yep
All rights reserved. No part of this book may be reproduced or utilized in any form or by any means, electronic or mechanical, including photocopying, recording or by any information storage and retrieval system, without permission in writing from the Publisher. Inquiries should be addressed to William Morrow and Company, Inc., 105 Madison Avenue, New York, N.Y. 10016.

Printed in the United States of America
10 9 8 7 6 5 4 3 2 1

Library of Congress Cataloging in Publication Data
Yep, Laurence. Liar, liar.
Summary: Branded in the past as a liar, a teen-aged boy trying to prove his friend's death in a car crash was no accident finds himself stalked by a seemingly respectable businessman for a similar fate.
[1. Murder—Fiction]
I. Title.   PZ7.Y44Li 1983   [Fic]   83-5432
ISBN 0-688-02417-3

To Uncle Francis and Auntie Rachel,
For their advice and support

1

I HAD TOLD MARSH THAT IT WAS DUMB TO MESS WITH THE gold Porsche. After all, we were right across the street from the Almaden police station, a one-story brick building that looked like a hamburger stand—as did most of the buildings in this city. I hadn't seen any cops around but that didn't mean one couldn't pop in or out at any time. In my opinion, it was just like asking for trouble.

Still, I would have done most anything for Marsh, and he'd have done the same for me. It had been that way ever since I'd moved into Almaden eight months ago and seen a half-dozen kids in Peterson High jackets surround him.

A kid with cheeks as round as a pumpkin's had pointed at Marsh. "That's the wise guy."

"Hello, Petey," Marsh had said calmly. "Come to visit your old neighborhood?"

"No," Petey had said, "we came to repay your favor."

It seemed that someone had unloaded a twenty-pound bag of fertilizer into the locker of their star quarterback before the big game with our school. And they had figured—rightly—that it could only have been Marsh, the biggest joker in all of Santa Clara County.

Even if he hadn't been my next-door neighbor, I think I would have helped out anyway. I hate long odds—maybe because I'm such an underdog myself.

Marsh had turned around to warn me. "You'd better stay out of this. Knights in shining armor are out of date nowadays."

I don't know what had gotten into me. Maybe I'd seen too many Burt Reynolds movies. I'd just raised my fists. "So maybe it's time to start a new fashion."

Or maybe not, as it turned out; because it hadn't taken those goons more than a few seconds to flatten both Marsh and me. But Marsh had played it cool, like he always did. There he was, flat on his back, blood streaming down from his nose, and he'd said, "Thanks. I couldn't have done this without your help." And then he'd given me one of his broad, lopsided grins.

And suddenly, I'd had this strange feeling—like I'd known him most of my life. I hadn't been able to figure it out until months later when I'd come across my old copy of *Tom Sawyer*. It was one of those illustrated volumes, and there, in the very first few pages, was a picture of Marsh—maybe a little younger and barefoot, but the same smile that said he didn't care about a thing in the world.

Marsh's grin had made me feel like everything was going to turn out okay after all. I'd done my best to shrug nonchalantly. "Hey, what are neighbors for?"

I never did find out what nasty treat the Peterson kids had in store for us because some of Marsh's friends had pulled up in a van the next moment. One of them, a big blonde kid named Howie, could lift the front of a Volkswagen Beetle all by himself. With him thundering at the head of the herd, it didn't take Marsh's friends long to send the Peterson kids running.

Marsh and I had been real tight after that. We'd done most everything together—including the answers to a quiz on *Huckleberry Finn*. But Ms. Semple had caught us, and now we had to write a thousand-word essay on why we shouldn't cheat.

And when we'd both copied the same article on ethics from an encyclopedia, she'd gotten even madder. She'd screwed up her nose like a fly had flown up a nostril and said we'd missed the whole point of the assignment; we had to do it all over again—and each of our essays had better be in our own words this time with the sources properly identified, and all that other stuff that teachers worry about.

So we had to waste a perfectly good April afternoon by staying cooped up in the library. It was after six by the time we finished and so we were feeling in a pretty foul mood.

But Marsh cheered up considerably when he saw the gold Porsche, in the vertical parking space right next to Marsh's own battered little Pinto.

"Well, well, well, look at who's come slumming," Marsh murmured. "I guess Semple wants to live dangerously."

I stepped off the sidewalk. "I thought she rode a broomstick."

"I guess she would if her husband wasn't some kind of hotshot salesman at a Porsche agency." He thrust his notebook into my hands.

"How do you know?" I pitched our notebooks through the open window onto the floor of the Pinto where our books already were.

"I overheard her bragging to some teachers one day." He surveyed the front of the Porsche with a critical eye. "It looks like it's riding a little high. Let's do our good deed for the day and let a little air out of the tires. What do you say?"

Expecting to see red lights flashing and sirens blowing, I glanced nervously over my shoulder at the police station; but there wasn't any sign of trouble—yet. "I say you're crazy. The cops are right across the street."

"I'm *inspired,*" he corrected me, "like Albert Einstein. Like Alexander the Great. Like Attila the Hun."

"Well, Attila, let's not conquer the world tonight. We've got that math quiz tomorrow." I pivoted around again and found him already crouching down by the right front wheel of the Porsche.

He started to unscrew the cap to the tire valve. "How can you expect to be the scourge of nations if you don't start practicing? Get the rear tire, will you? She'll have one spare tire, but not two."

"But how can you be sure this is her car?" I almost put my fingers against the sides before I remembered that I might leave fingerprints.

Marsh threw the cap underneath the car. "I'm the one who put glue in her locks. I ought to know my own victims." He dug a paper clip out of his pocket and began to straighten it out. "Why all this static? Don't tell me you're trying to protect her."

"Me? Don't be stupid." The last thing I wanted to do was to fall out with Marsh over someone like Ms. Semple, so I retreated toward the rear of the car and squatted down.

"You're going to need one of these too." Marsh poked around at the valve with the wire until, with a sudden flick of his wrist, the wire opened something and we could hear the telltale hiss. "There's a little thing in the tire valve that keeps the air from leaking out. So we have to jam it open."

I chucked the cap away and began to search my pockets but couldn't find a clip of my own. "Have you got another one of those things?"

But, as always, Marsh was thinking one step ahead of me. He had already straightened out another paper clip. "One fiendish device coming up." He duck-walked back to me and presented it to me with a flourish.

I had just stuck the clip into the valve when I heard a man call out angrily. "Hey, what are you doing to my car?"

"I turned to see a big, middle-aged, bald-headed man running toward us. "You simp," I said to Marsh, "this isn't her car."

"I would have sworn this was the same car. Maybe that guy's her husband." Marsh got out his car keys as he stood up.

"Maybe," I said, "but he doesn't look like he wants to chat about his family."

"Yeah, let's get out of here." Marsh jumped into the

driver's seat; and, for once, the engine started on the first try. But, since I had to head around to the rear of the car to reach the passenger's side, it meant I had to go around behind Marsh's car. And that was when I noticed the funny thing about the Porsche. It had a large, faded orange-daisy decal on the trunk. And that's not something you expect to find on your typical Porsche.

"You punks think you can get away with anything, don't you." The guy was only fifty feet away now and he looked like he would have cheerfully stomped us into the ground and mailed our remains COD to our folks.

I didn't even bother opening the door but dove headfirst through the open window on the passenger's side.

"Five-four-three...." Marsh was counting down to blast-off time. I was still in the process of drawing my legs through the window when Marsh shouted, "Zero! Blast-off!" And backed out of the space with a screech.

But I was still half in, half out of the car. "Slow down. I don't want to break my neck."

"I can't," Marsh laughed in nervous excitement. "He's coming." His foot slammed against the brake pedal, but even so the car kept rolling slowly backwards. Like the rest of Marsh's car, the brake system was old and worn.

"Well, don't run him over." I managed to draw my legs in so that my knees were now on the seat. I half expected to hear the crunch of metal as Marsh backed into some other car. "I hope your insurance is paid up."

"Insurance? What's that?" Marsh shifted into first gear and swung the wheel sharply, sending the car tearing toward the exit.

As I pulled myself up so that I was now kneeling on the seat, I looked out the rear window. The man was standing by the Porsche, but he wasn't inspecting his car. He was busy staring at us. His eyes were so intense that they might as well have been radar. I could almost feel the invisible waves beaming at us. As Marsh hung a screeching right turn out of the lot, I saw the man take out a pen and scribble something on a scrap of paper.

2

"WE'RE IN BI-I-IG TROUBLE, MARSH." I SLUMPED DOWN against the seat. "I think he got your license plate."

"So what?" Marsh adjusted the rearview mirror. "It's just his word against ours." He leaned his elbow out the window, steering with just the fingertips of his right hand. To look at Marsh, you'd think he didn't have a care in the world. "Besides, even if he could prove something, it'd just be a fine for malicious mischief. The worst that could happen to us is that our folks would have to go down and talk to the judge." He bit his lower lip thoughtfully for a moment and then added, "Though come to think of it, I'd rather face jail than my father."

"You don't know jail," I said meaningfully.

"You don't know my father." Marsh punched a button on his radio. "He's an ex-marine." When the radio didn't go on, he hammered a fist against the dashboard. "C'mon, you pile of junk." When it still didn't go on, he sighed. "Well, it was always more static than music anyway."

Actually, Marsh's Pinto could be called a car only in the loosest sense of the word. When one thing wasn't going wrong, it was always another. If the door wasn't jammed, then the thermostat was broken or the windshield wipers would break and go flying into the air. Actually, I was glad Marsh had reminded me that his car was a junk heap; in the rush to escape the Porsche driver, I'd forgotten my usual precaution of buckling up.

"Funny," I said, searching for the seat belt, "your dad doesn't look like the marine type."

"He washed out." Marsh turned to leer at me. "He was a psycho."

I finally realized I was being fooled once again. "Yeah, well, I can see his son's a chip off the old block."

He eyed the seat belt in my hand. "That's right," he said, "buckle up for safety like a good little puppet."

"Don't start that again." I really hated it when he gave me grief. "How many times do I have to tell you that there aren't any strings on me?"

"You scare me sometimes, Sean." His face took on a sad, serious look. "You're smart enough to know there are strings even if you can't see them." He swung the car east onto Avalon, a broad street of low, windowless buildings like so many plastic Lego blocks. It was the part of northern California known as Silicon Valley that swept in one long, continuous band through several cities. There, in bright, dustless rooms, the workers made the silicon chips for all those dandy home computers, video games, digital watches and smart bombs.

"You're just like all the other kids. You sit around whining about how boring your parents are," he continued, "but you'll wind up making chips here just like them."

"This place isn't so bad."

"Grow up, Sean." He hung a sudden, screeching left out of the rush-hour traffic onto Camelot Lane so that we were now driving through a tract of ranch houses. "Why do you think they give all those fancy names to the streets?" His voice rose as he got caught up in the idea. "Look at our school. We talk to *career consultants,* not counselors. And we read books in a *media center,* not a school library. And for all I know we'll be drinking water out of a *hydraulic interface,* not a fountain." He slapped a hand down firmly against the wheel. "We've got to destroy all the labels and the strings."

I began to poke at the buttons of the radio, trying to drown out Marsh's talk. A serious Marsh was twice as crazy as a joking Marsh. "So how come you wear that pair of jeans with the fancy label on the back pocket?"

It was hard for Marsh to stay serious for long. The old familiar grin snapped back into place. "They're just camouflage so that the puppets won't know I'm different." He tapped the side of his nose. "I'm Pinocchio in disguise."

I pretended to drop my mouth open in surprise. "You mean all this time that I thought you were just another practical joker, you were actually a guerrilla for the Puppet Liberation Front?"

Marsh held up a finger to his lips and said in a hushed,

saccharine voice, "And the blue fairy's promised me that if I keep this up, one day I can become a *real* boy."

I didn't have any better luck with the radio than Marsh. "Well, this is one fight I think I'm going to sit out."

Marsh shook his head sadly, as if I had just confessed to liking Donny Osmond records. "If you don't go looking for the war, the war will come looking for you."

Tires squealing, he accelerated around the corner into the cul-de-sac that some genius had named Corbenic Court. Another sharp right sent us thumping onto the driveway of his house. The garage door seemed to leap toward us before he hit the brakes and we came to a halt. Barely.

Maybe it was all that bouncing around or maybe it was just whatever imp controlled the radio, but it chose that precise moment to snap on, filling the air with a loud New Wave song.

Marsh laughed at me because I had my legs braced against the floorboards and my hands on the dashboard. "I was in complete control, Sean." He turned off the radio.

"Well, I wish you'd get your pilot's license before you take off again. You would have made a great kamikaze."

The sound of someone typing came from the second story of Marsh's house. "Your sister must be home." Nora was a year younger than Marsh and a sophomore. She was always writing some really heavy article for the school newspaper about pollution or nuclear disarmament.

Marsh frowned up at the window. "Yeah. It must be hard being the conscience of the entire world, but she's giving it a good try." He kicked one of his tires. "You know what she watches on TV for fun?"

I gathered my books up from the floor of the car. "I

can't wait to find out."

"A presidential news conference." He shook his head. "She just sits and hoots all the time. And then she dashes upstairs to write a bunch of angry letters." Marsh pantomimed someone typing furiously. She even looked up what *Corbenic* meant."

I piled my things on my lap. "I thought it was just another one of those Indian names used to torture poor spellers."

Marsh got out of the car. "No, it's the castle where the Holy Grail was kept."

"The what?" I looked at him blankly.

"It's a special cup that King Arthur and his knights were always looking for." He stretched elaborately.

I didn't actually know Nora too well because she was either in her room or en route to some Concerned Students meeting. But from what Marsh had told me she sounded like his complete opposite. "Are you sure she's your sister?"

"I'm having detectives check into it." Marsh shrugged. "But you know how parents get attached to things—like old chairs and stuff. She's just gotten so familiar that I'm afraid they're going to keep her around anyway." He heaved a big, melodramatic sigh. "When my folks asked me if I wanted a baby brother or sister, I told them a pony would be a lot easier." He arched his eyebrows. "And I was right."

"They say a prophet's never appreciated in his own home."

"Say." Marsh closed his door. "What was that you said about jail?"

"What do you mean?" I nudged the door so that it

swung slowly across its hinges, gathering momentum until it slammed shut.

"You said something about my not knowing what jail was like. What do you know about it?"

"I was just joking." There was no way I was going to confess something like that to Marsh. I might find the news splashed on a banner hung over our school some day.

Marsh leaned against his car. "It's an odd sort of joke."

"So I'll memorize some joke books." Before he could question me any further, I crossed his driveway and skirted the huge bottle bush that separated our two houses.

3

I HEADED STRAIGHT FOR THE KITCHEN WHEN I GOT HOME. I needed to talk to someone—as much about some of the things Marsh had said as about the Porsche driver. It was times like these that I really wished Mom and Dad could have stayed together.

I took the receiver off the kitchen phone and dialed Mom's number up in Seattle. While it rang, I took a couple of deep breaths and tried to think of what to tell Mom and how to say it. I didn't use to plan my conversations with Mom, but that was five years ago, before she had taken my little sister, Caitlin, to Seattle and left me behind with Dad. I told myself it was dumb; but sometimes I had the feeling that she couldn't wait to run away from me—the way some families abandon a stupid, ugly pet when they move away.

When I heard someone pick up the receiver at the other end, I said as cheerfully as I could, "How're you doing?"

"Fine," a man said. It was Neil, Mom's friend. He wasn't exactly the smartest person in the world. In fact, his brains were so small that they probably rattled whenever he did jumping jacks. But, as Caitlin said, he had a great bod. Still, it had disappointed me that my mother would go for someone like that. I would have hoped she'd have had higher standards.

But he seemed to make Mom happy so I had to get along with him. I tried to keep the warmth in my voice; but it sounded strained, even to me. "Hello, Neil. This is Sean. Can I talk to my mom?"

Neil's cheerfulness was equally as thin. I think he had as much use for me as I had for him. "Oh, hi, Sean. She's in the shower right now, but I'll have her call you as soon as she gets out."

I felt this sudden little flash of anger that made me want to ask him what business it was of his to be there while Mom was taking a shower, but I kept my mouth shut.

When I had visited Mom last summer and met Neil, I'd tried to give him the sullen, silent treatment until Mom had sat me down and very gently but firmly explained a modernized version of the facts of life—mainly that I ought to be mature enough to realize that she had her own life to live now.

It doesn't matter why Neil's with Mom, I told myself. It just doesn't matter. So keep hold of your temper.

"Well," I said, trying to sound casual, "is Caitlin there?"

"No," Neil said, "she's sleeping over at a friend's place."

"So it's just you and me on the phone, is it?" It was a dumb joke, but I was trying to stall for time until Mom got out of the shower.

"Yeah." He gave a nervous little laugh. "I guess it is." He paused and then added. "So how are the Giants doing?"

I had to give Neil points for trying. Guys are supposed to have a great time talking about baseball. Only I didn't know zilch.

So, instead, I threw in a sentence I heard a lot at school. "They just don't have the hitting."

"Isn't that always the way?" Neil sighed. "And when they have the hitting, they don't have the pitching." There was a long, awkward silence that Neil finally broke. "Well, I'll have her call you as soon as she's out," he promised.

But I felt real guilty right then for calling up Mom at the first sign of trouble. After all, I wasn't a little kid anymore. And when I thought about it, there really wasn't too much she could do to help me anyway. Besides, with Caitlin gone, she and Neil probably had a big evening planned. There was no sense spoiling it by having me rambling on about nothing.

"No, don't bother," I said. "I just called to see how she was doing."

"You're sure?" Neil asked a little sharply.

And suddenly I wondered just how much Mom had told him about me. "I'm fine." I tried to sound as positive as I could.

"Okay," he said cautiously. "Take care of yourself, Sean."

"Right, right," I muttered, and hung up.

Of course, Dad got on my case as soon as I left the kitchen. "Hey, sport," he called from his study.

I walked down the hallway to his room. It was almost wall to wall with technical manuals. Occupying one wall was Dad's home terminal that was hooked by phone to the ones at his company. He was always trying to get me to use it by telling me how much fun computer programming was. But I could remember all those late nights when he was grumbling over some program that he just couldn't debug. Right at that moment, he was sitting at his desk using a wide sheet of computer printout as scrap paper.

"It's almost seven, sport. Where have you been?" Dad capped his felt-tip pen and set it in the little office caddy where all his other pens and pencils were neatly arrayed like missiles.

"Studying." I leaned against the doorway. "Do you want an affidavit or can I just show you my homework?"

Dad twisted around in his chair. "I'm sure you've got proof. But couldn't it have waited until after you took care of the bottle bush?" Dad had been after me for months to trim the thing. "After all, we had a contract."

The idea for the contract was Dad's, not mine—as if running the household and raising me were just like a business. Ever since he'd split up with Mom, Dad had been clipping the home and household articles from the newspaper on how to cope with kids, rats and other disasters.

The only trouble with our contract was that Dad treated me less like an employee than his slave. Employees, at least, get a definite list of duties; but Dad kept adding on to my list. It had become almost a point of honor with me not to trim the bush. "I don't know. I think it adds a nice natural touch to the house."

"It's spreading over both our driveway and the Weisses'." Dad waved his hand as if the bottle bush were going to come crashing through our front door at any moment. "I'm going to dock three dollars from your allowance until you get around to doing it. If you want to be treated as my equal, you're going to have to do an equal amount of work."

Dad believed in democracy about as much as a South American general did. I was only his equal in the household as long as I did what he said. "What did that bush ever do to you, Dad?"

"Come on, sport," Dad coaxed. "Who wins the long-distance race?"

It was one of Dad's favorite quotes from one of his running magazines. "Not the lean one," I said with a smile. If Dad noticed I was kidding him, he didn't say anything.

Dad leaned his head back. "And not the fast one."

"And not the dirty one."

We both chimed in together. "It's the disciplined one."

Dad beamed. "You've got to be organized, sport. Or you'll never get anywhere."

I wondered if Dad realized how ironic this sounded coming from him. About six years ago, Dad had tried to start up his own computer-software company. It hadn't taken long for the company to go belly up. So he'd had to swallow his pride and go to work for a man fifteen years his junior. Dad specialized now in troubleshooting computer programs.

I could see he was busy. Even so, I really felt like keeping the conversation going. I went over to the desk and pointed to the flow chart on it. "Having problems?"

"Just having to debug this new program." Dad dismissed it with a wave of his hand as if it was nothing.

"I couldn't make heads or tails of it. You might just as well have asked me to give you street directions for a house in New Delhi. "It looks hard to me."

Dad stood up and stretched. "The Kid says that there's something wrong with it." The Kid was what Dad called his boss. "Though I'd swear it must be the operator's fault." He shook his head. "I don't think the Kid would know how to turn on a computer unless someone showed him how." Then a new thought occurred to him. "So who drove you home?"

"Marsh," I said.

Dad frowned as if he'd just bitten into a sour dill pickle. "Don't you have any other friends?"

"Marsh has a car." I stiffened, getting ready for another lecture on how to run life's race.

"I don't want you hanging around with that boy. He's poison." Dad spread his arms. "I thought we agreed. No mistakes like last time."

"I won't get into trouble," I promised him.

"You've got to change, Sean."

"What, Dad? Underwear? Morals?"

"You know perfectly well what I mean." He tapped his fingers impatiently on the desk top. "We agreed that you were going to change your attitude."

"That's right. A new house. A new school. A new city." I started to turn away. "Too bad it's not a new me."

"Wait, sport." When I was facing him again, Dad clasped his hands. "I'm not doing this right at all."

It's funny. You could ask Dad to set up a program to

send a rocket to Pluto and he wouldn't blink an eye. But asking him to really listen to someone was like asking him to cut his own throat. He never did it well.

"Don't worry about it."

"But I do, sport." Dad spread his hands as if he were trying to grasp a gigantic vase and found it heavier than he thought. "What you think *is* important to me. I just may not always show it all the time. I get . . . distracted."

"Hey," I said quietly, "I know that, Dad. You're busy with your job."

Dad got these twitches of conscience every now and then and that meant I was in for another fishing trip. They wouldn't have been so bad if Dad hadn't been so determined to have fun. We'd be out in the stream casting our lines even if it was raining hard enough to start building another ark. Dad cleared his throat. "We'll do something together. . . ."

"As soon as you catch up on your projects," I finished for him.

Dad frowned. "How did you know what I was going to say?" He gave a sniff. "Do I say it that often?"

I shrugged. "Not that much."

He studied me. "You're getting taller, aren't you? In two years, you'll be leaving for college."

I tried to grin. "Making your plans to rent out my room already?"

He put his hand on my shoulder. As a family we didn't touch much or even kiss, so it was odd to feel the warmth in Dad's hand. "I promise you that we'll go off. Maybe make a trip around the country. Would you like that?"

"Sure." I brightened. I'd never been out of the state once in my whole life, which had been embarrassing at one time. At my last school, a lot of the kids had been on trips as far away as Europe; and they were always going skiing in Colorado or some other place.

"We'll have fun," Dad said.

"Unless you get a better job and have to start over at a new company." It was a mean thing to say.

Dad dropped his hand. "Even if I do . . ." his voice trailed off. We both knew what his priorities would be.

"Yeah, let's do something together when you have the time, Dad." I was really sorry that I had broken the contact between us. It had been like a short, bright little spark. "Well." I held up my books and binder. "I'd better finish my homework."

"Yes." Dad almost seemed relieved when he turned back to his desk. "And I've got work to do myself."

I retreated down the hallway toward the stairs that went to my room on the second floor.

It's strange how we always used the same excuse to get away from one another.

4

TWO WEEKS LATER, I STILL HAD THIS JUMPY FEELING ABOUT the Porsche driver. Nothing had happened in the meantime. No cops had broken down my door. I hadn't even gotten so much as an angry phone call. But I couldn't help thinking about that guy again when we went to a midnight showing of the *Rocky Horror Picture Show*. Marsh said it was a fine send-up of American culture, but I had my doubts. It's hard for me to take seriously a movie where the alien wears a corset. Well, anyway, the alien's assistant was this bald-headed guy with this real intense stare—like he was figuring out the best way to zap you. And his eyes reminded me of the Porsche driver's.

As I got into Marsh's car, I couldn't help asking, "Don't you think it's wierd that the guy at the library hasn't done anything yet?"

Marsh started the car and swung it toward one of the many exits in the theater's parking lot. "You're going to get an ulcer before you're twenty." He snapped on the radio. For a change, it worked. "The guy may have been mad, but he just figured that there was nothing he could do to us."

"But you didn't see his look, Marsh." I circled my hands around my eyes to emphasize my point. "He had these... these radar eyes."

"What's with you, Sean?" Marsh threw up a weary, disgusted hand. "Do you like being anxious and miserable? Is that it? I would've forgotten all about it, but you had to remind me."

"I can't help it if I have a good memory." I leaned my head back against the seat.

"Do you see what I meant about invisible strings? You'll never learn to be happy until you cut them." Marsh swung his Pinto onto Stevens Creek.

"I'm happy enough." I squirmed in my seat because some rice had gotten underneath my shirt collar and it was sticking to the wet fabric. (We'd made the mistake of sitting in front of some bozo with a shopping bag full of toast, rice and squirt guns.)

"Wait a moment," Marsh said. "This is my favorite song." And he cranked the sound up so that it filled the Pinto and most of the street too.

Five songs later, he was still hopping up and down in time to the music as he turned onto the expressway. It was a broad, six-lane road where the speed limit was forty-five and there were only a few traffic lights to slow you down. Since it was nearly two o'clock on Sunday morning, the expressway was deserted except for us.

I started to close my eyes but then I saw how the needle of the speedometer leapt quickly from thirty to forty-five and then to fifty. Ahead of us, a green traffic light changed to yellow; Marsh picked up speed on the empty expressway.

When the DJ finally came back on to plug some products, Marsh turned down the radio again and glanced over at me, ready to resume our conversation.

"You only think you're happy because that's what everyone tells you," Marsh explained. "But you don't know what this wicked world is really like. You've got to move like a porpoise sliding through a sea full of light." As if to emphasize his point, Marsh pressed his foot on the accelerator pedal so that we were hitting sixty by the time we roared through the intersection.

"Congratulations." I buckled myself in. "You've managed to make it through a yellow light."

The music came on again and Marsh turned it up. "They're showing *The Blob* on the tube tonight. If we hurry, we can just make it." He leaned his left elbow out the window and began beating time on the car roof to the music on the radio."

"What's *The Blob*?" I asked suspiciously.

"You never saw the funniest horror movie of all time?" Marsh shook his head at my ignorance. "It's all about this kid who discovers a monster, but no one will believe him. The Blob looks like someone dumped a bottle of ketchup into a pot of mush and then let it boil over. I just love it."

I didn't have a bug about monster movies like Marsh

had. But I didn't feel like another lecture. I settled back in the seat, planning to sleep through most of the movie.

The expressway seemed to stretch on forever into the clear, spring night. Up above, the sky seemed as black as the asphalt of the road. You couldn't see any stars at all because of the glare from the street lights. I had the eerie feeling that we'd never get off the expressway, that it would just go on and on past silent shopping malls and darkened houses. The car would never run out of gas and never have to stop and we'd just go soaring up finally into that dark, endless sky.

Far away, a traffic light winked from yellow to red and the mood was broken. "Well," I said drowsily, "this is one light we're not going to make."

But Marsh didn't ease up on the accelerator. "Sometimes the lights change back."

Ahead of us, I could make out the intersection. There were traffic lights on all four corners and on the islands in the middle of the expressway. To the left was a gasoline station and to the right was a realtor's. "Slow down, Marsh. You never know where a cop might be hiding."

"You're a real joy to go cruising with, you know that?" Marsh growled at me. He lifted his foot from the accelerator and brought it down on the brake pedal. The car gave a little jerk from the right to the left.

I straightened up. "Come on, Marsh. Don't make a joke out of it."

"I'm not." He jerked his head toward the back. "The front brakes are holding but something's gone wrong with the rear ones." Bracing his left foot on the floor of the car, Marsh jammed his right foot down so hard on the brake pedal that he rose from his seat.

"Try the hand brake." I started to reach for it.

Marsh grunted, "I got it."

My hands were gripping the dashboard tightly and my right foot was pressing against the floorboard as if there were a brake pedal there. And I was willing the car to stop ... please stop.

Finally, the car began to slow; then almost at the same instant it began to swerve from side to side as if it were a salmon wriggling upriver. Red lights flashed on the instrument panel as the engine stalled, but our momentum carried us forward relentlessly.

Car crashes aren't fun like they are on TV.

As the car started to turn over, I just wouldn't believe it. Instead, I thought the whole world had gone crazy; the street had suddenly swung overhead and the sky seemed to be underneath us. I told myself that this was happening to someone else—not to me.

The windshield shattered into hundreds of little bits of glass that looked like drops of water in a fountain and the metal of the roof screeched as we skidded along the expressway. When we finally came to a halt, the car hood was nosed into the street like a plow.

But finally there I was hanging upside down in the car seat with only the seat belt to support me. Even when I released the seat belt and wound up on the ceiling of the car, it still seemed more like a nightmare than reality.

The car was as dark as a coffin. All I could think of was getting out of there, so I slid through the open window of the car. I expected to see Marsh already on his feet and swearing at the Pinto, but there wasn't any sign of him.

When I heard the ominous rumbling, I turned and saw a truck about a hundred yards away moving toward us fast. It looked like some huge, humpbacked metal beast with large glowing eyes and it was charging straight toward us without any sign of slowing down. Maybe the driver was sleepy or maybe he just thought we were slow leaving the green light.

I started to wave my hands frantically at the truck while I called out, "Marsh, where are you?"

There was no response. Frightened, I got down on a knee and looked through the window. "Quit kidding around, Marsh. There's a truck coming."

But Marsh just lay there on the crumbled roof of the car, his legs tucked behind him neatly, one arm flung out through the broken windshield. He might have been asleep—if it hadn't been for the fact that his neck was bent back at that crazy angle, the way no neck should be.

I could feel the truck rumbling down on me, the lights splashing brightly around the car. I glanced up. I could just make out the truck-driver's face. He seemed to have woken up from whatever daydream he was having. His mouth fell open and his hand slapped loudly at his horn. He hit his brakes and there was a grinding, screeching sound.

And I knew I couldn't wait for Marsh anymore. I turned and dove for the curb and when I hit the asphalt I went rolling.

It seemed to take forever for the truck to hit Marsh's car, but when it did, there was a sickening crunching sound and a sudden burst of light so that it seemed as bright as day. And then I heard the sound of the explosion and felt the sudden blast of heat. I flopped over onto my stomach.

The impact had shoved the Pinto into the middle of the intersection. The truck driver had leapt from the high cab of his truck, but the Pinto itself was a flaming ball of metal. I scrambled to my feet and ran toward the car. The truck driver appeared and grabbed my arm.

He looked as scared as me, but he held me firmly. "You can't go in there," he said.

I fought and twisted. "My pal's in that car."

"He's not alive anymore," the driver said as the flames went roaring even higher.

My legs felt like jelly, and I suddenly sank to my knees. "Marsh," I called to the car. "Marsh!"

5

THE EMERGENCY ROOM AT THE HOSPITAL TREATED MY CUTS, scrapes and bruises, but they were minor. The hard part was facing Dad.

He was leaning against a wall in the waiting room. The hem of his pajama top peeked out from underneath the jacket as if he had just thrown on his clothes. He shoved himself upright when he saw me. "What happened, sport?"

Since the accident, my brain seemed to have disconnected itself from my body. When I tried to tell Dad about the accident, it seemed to be with someone else's lips.

"We were on the expressway ... in Marsh's car. We wanted to stop. But the brakes went and we flipped over. But I made it out okay."

I don't know why Dad and I never had heart-to-heart talks like other people did. We didn't mean to hurt one another but we always managed to. My old shrink used to say that was because we really didn't understand one another. He used to say that Dad and I were like two blind bears. When we meant to give the other a love pat, we wound up cutting him instead.

At any rate, Dad's relief changed almost instantly into anger. "Didn't I tell you what would happen if you hung around with that boy?"

"That boy is ... was ... my friend and he's...." And suddenly my old reliable tongue froze up on me. "He's...." But I just couldn't bring myself to finish the sentence and say that Marsh was dead.

Dad ran a hand over his face. "I shouldn't have spoken like that." He had a real sorrowful look on his face. "But I just get so mad at you for taking risks. Why do you have to scare me like that?"

"It wasn't intentional," I mumbled.

"I tell you what. In a few days when you're feeling better, we'll go look for that tape deck you've been wanting." He started to put his arm around my shoulder.

I stepped away. The last thing I wanted right then was to have him pawing me and using all that sentimental stuff to criticize me even more. "Why do you think you have to bribe me all the time?"

Dad's arm was still hanging in the air. He dropped it

now—almost resentfully. "I was just trying to show you I was sorry."

"So money always makes things okay?" I sneered.

Dad's eyes narrowed like he wanted to give me one of his lectures about respecting him. Instead, he just pressed his lips together, filing the lecture away for later when I was in better shape. "Right, sport," was all he said. And then, his back rigid and his shoulders squared like a martyr walking to the lions, he started for the doors.

It didn't occur to me until we were outside the hospital that I would have to ride in another car to get home. I looked at the parking lot. Even that early in the morning there were two or three dozen cars. The light from the streetlamps glinted off their tops.

And suddenly I felt very cold and alone. The tall hospital towered over me, making me feel the size of an ant, and above the hospital was the black night sky looking so big and far away.

"Something wrong?" Dad's keys clinked as he took them from his pocket.

I lowered my head defensively. I was afraid to give Dad an excuse to start scolding me again about the accident and how stupid I was. "Let's just get out of here before they claim me for spare parts."

He let me open my own door and I slid into the Chevy. It was like a big metal whale compared to Marsh's Pinto. But even the Chevy felt dangerous now—especially when Dad turned on the ignition. I mean, once Marsh and I thought nothing would ever happen to us. No matter how bad the accident, we would walk away from it just like Burt Reynolds always does. Only I knew now that it didn't work that way in real life.

I wasn't about to scream and jump out of the car, but I felt like the real me had withdrawn even further away from my body so that there was just an old husk sitting in the front seat of Dad's car.

Dad took it slower than he would have normally. I sensed that and was grateful, but I was too far away to come back to thank him. Anyway, we were never big on calling attention to what we did for one another. Only on what we didn't do.

When we got home, Dad insisted that I call Mom up in Seattle. I wasn't too crazy about the idea because my mood wasn't going to be helped any if Neil answered it. But it was Mom who answered. "Sean?" she panted.

I held the receiver away from my ear and stared at it for a moment. "How come you're out of breath?"

"I've been put on the night shift at the center. I was just coming in the door." Mom worked as a counselor at a suicide prevention center up in Seattle. "But what's your excuse for being up so early."

"So late," I corrected her.

Her voice grew real soft and gentle. "What's happened, Sean?"

Under normal circumstances, I liked talking to Mom, but I was still in a state of shock. So I gave her the *Reader's Digest* condensed version. "I was in a car crash but I'm okay."

"Thank Heaven," Mom said fervently.

"But my friend...." My tongue suddenly quit on me again, but I forced myself to go on. "My friend's dead."

"Was it Marsh?"

My voice broke, but I still managed a hoarse "Yes."

There was a pause and then Mom asked, "Would you like to talk about it?"

And it was as if someone had put my brain into neutral. I just couldn't get it to function. "No, not now."

"Maybe it's too soon," Mom agreed. "But you feel free to call me anytime. You've got my number at work?"

I flipped open our address book. "Yeah."

"Well," Mom urged as gently as she could, "write it down on a slip of paper and feel free to call me there. Phone collect if you want."

I nodded my head numbly. "Yeah, sure." I wrote the number down quickly. "I didn't wake Caitlin, did I?"

"No, you know what a sound sleeper she is," Mom said.

"A regular buzz saw." I tucked the number away in my jeans. "So look. I'm sorry to keep you up. And I'll call you the first thing when I'm feeling better."

"Or not," Mom instructed me.

"Or not," I repeated. I started to hang up the receiver but Dad shook his hand.

"No, I want a word with your mother," he said, reaching out for the receiver.

"Why? Need some semiprofessional advice on how to handle me?" I handed the phone over to Dad and left the kitchen as he started to talk to Mom.

All I wanted to do was retreat up to Idaho. That was the nickname Marsh had given my bedroom because it reminded him of the B-52's song. He'd said that it was my own personal wasteland where I hid. But I cut off those thoughts. I didn't want to start thinking about Marsh and all the things he'd said.

I just wanted to sleep for a week. Maybe the whole thing would turn out to be a bad dream. Or maybe if I could sleep long enough, I would wake up one morning feeling healthy and whole again.

The only problem with that strategy is that the world

refuses to leave you alone. Dad woke me around noon to tell me that the police wanted to talk to me. I sat up sleepily, blinking my eyes, and feeling just as bad as I had before. "Can't I do it some other day?" I looked at Dad, pleading silently with him to do me a favor just this once.

But Dad had turned his back and was headed out the door. "You just might as well get it over with," he said.

I sighed. Dad and I always seemed to miss our signals. And anyway, Dad was big on cooperating with the law.

When I came into the living room, I found a broad, heavily built policeman. He introduced himself as Lieutenant Silva and told me he had just a few questions to ask.

"Sure." Nervously I knotted the belt to my bathrobe and sat down next to him on the sofa.

Lieutenant Silva's notebook was already open on his left palm. He jotted something down quickly and then glanced at me again. "Why don't you tell me what happened, Sean?"

I cleared my throat. It was a little easier to talk about it now that I'd had a few hours of sleep. "Well, we were driving along when we saw the light change. Marsh hit the brakes—only something went wrong. The rear brakes wouldn't work. We kind of fishtailed"—I pantomimed with my hand for emphasis—"and suddenly we flipped over." My voice lowered. "I had on my seat belt but Marsh didn't."

Suddenly, I felt myself filled with an overwhelming sense of shame because I'd run out on Marsh and left him to die. "His neck was at a funny angle so I think it was broken." It was important for everyone to know that.

"Otherwise I would have tried to pull him out. His neck was broken, wasn't it?" I couldn't help asking.

Lieutenant Silva looked at me sympathetically as if he knew what I was going through, but he was careful to keep his voice distant and controlled. "We won't know until the autopsy."

He consulted his notebook again. "Now how fast would you say your friend was driving?"

"Fifty-five. Maybe sixty." I wouldn't look at Dad.

"Did your friend ever have trouble with the brakes before this?"

I had to admit, "They weren't any too good."

"I don't want to speak ill of the dead," Dad spoke up from his armchair, "but Marsh didn't help those brakes any. His dad was always complaining about the speeding tickets he collected." Dad clasped his hands over his lap. "He used to take the corner on two wheels and a prayer. It's a wonder the brake system didn't fail earlier."

"Fail?" I asked.

"You see, sport," Dad explained, "there's a master cylinder that supplies half of its fluid to the front brakes and half to the rear ones. Now the rear brake line could have ruptured because it was old or just worn out. And if the rear brakes failed but the front ones worked, the car would swing around and flip over just as Marsh's car did—if you were driving fast enough."

Lieutenant Silva had already closed his notebook as if that was his own opinion too. But it just didn't seem right to me that they could write off Marsh's death so easily. It was all too smug and pat. Dad made it sound almost as if Marsh had deserved to die.

"Is that it?" I asked in protest. My hands shaped the big

letters of a newspaper headline. "Crazy Kid Kills Self."

Lieutenant Silva paused in the act of putting away his notebook into his shirt pocket. "What makes you think it wasn't an accident?"

Well, if it wasn't an accident, what was it then? Murder? I told myself not to be crazy. Things like that didn't happen in nice, clean suburban Almaden.

6

ALL THE REST OF THAT SUNDAY THE CAR CRASH KEPT COMING back to me. I would be walking around the house or just eating a sandwich at the table or watching some TV show and suddenly, for no reason I could think of, I'd be back in Marsh's old rattletrap car, feeling how it vibrated and clanked along, and still hear Marsh drumming his fingers to the beat of the radio's music.

And I'd remember the screech of the brakes and Marsh's panicked voice and the world would turn upside down again; and I'd watch the buildings and streetlights spin the wrong way and then the car roof would begin to screech again. I'd call to Marsh in the silence, but there wouldn't be any answer. And meanwhile, in the distance would be the steadily growing rumble of a truck.

It didn't seem right—not right at all—that Lieutenant Silva and Dad and all the other people would shrug off the car crash as just an accident. They almost made it sound as if Marsh had been asking to die. After all, a unique human life had been lost and couldn't be replaced. We ought to do more than shrug it off and go on as if nothing had happened. But if I wanted the lieutenant to put more energy into his investigation, I was going to have to come up with something.

I tossed and turned most of the night trying to figure out a new angle on things that might change the lieutenant's mind. But the idea didn't hit me until Monday morning. Marsh had played so many jokes on people that maybe someone had decided to get even by tampering with the brakes so that Marsh would have a good scare—only the prank had gotten out of hand. But what sort of things could you do to the brake system?

I didn't know and at first I wasn't sure how to find out. It's not the kind of casual question you can ask at any gas station. Then I remembered Howie. He tinkered with cars and had, in fact, helped Marsh with the Pinto a few times. I rolled over in my bed to look at the clock. It was only eight in the morning. Dad would already have left for work, but I had plenty of time to get to school for first period PE. And I'd find Howie there.

It was a weird experience to bicycle onto campus—like wandering into someone else's dream. The kids were laughing and smiling and flirting as if no one had died.

I headed for the big bronze statue of a miner from the

Almaden Quicksilver Mines. The whole area used to be rotten with mercury ore at one time, though I supposed it had all been used up by then. At least, I hoped so. Marsh had told me that mercury vapors could drive people crazy—like the Mad Hatter in Alice in Wonderland because hatters used to need mercury when they made beaver hats.

The bike racks stood in the shadow of the statue; and all the bicycles there reminded me of giant insects feeding at a trough. I stowed mine among them and started to look for Howie, when I heard a girl call, "I think it's terrible about Marsh."

I turned to see Gina, a plump little brunette with enough metal in her braces to build a bridge. We'd gone out a couple of times on double dates with Marsh. She was busy winding a heavy chain through the spokes of her imported racing bike.

I rested my hands on the cool, reassuring metal of my bike. "The car just flipped over."

"Ugh." She grimaced.

"I would have gone back for Marsh." It was important that Gina know I didn't desert Marsh. "But the car caught on fire."

"Double ugh." Gina looked a little sick at the thought of it.

I suppose I should have shut up right then, but I had to make it clear to her that it wasn't my fault that Marsh was dead. I don't think I spoke for more than a few minutes, but maybe it was longer. Even when Gina started to fidget as if she was getting nervous, I couldn't stop myself.

Maybe I would have still been talking if a blonde girl hadn't come running over. "Gina," she screeched, as her long hair flew around behind her. She stopped when she saw me. "Oh, hello, Sean. It's awful about Marsh, isn't it?"

"Yes," I said and was going to begin all over again when Gina made a point of grabbing the blonde's hands.

She raised her eyebrows, a half smile playing around her lips. "You'll never guess what I saw."

The blonde placed her hand over Gina's. "You mean Sabrina?"

Gina gave a laugh and nodded. "You saw her in those slacks?"

The blonde giggled. "She calls them puce."

"More like puke." Gina laughed again.

"Excuse me," I said coldly. Gina nodded with relief as I wandered away. I wondered whether they were going to gossip now about Sabrina or me.

The other kids were just like that. At first they all made the proper noises about Marsh and mugged sympathetically, but it didn't take long before they made their excuses and got away from me.

It bothered me—though I couldn't say why until I met the Can Man. He was this old guy who actually shouldn't have been on campus; but no one complained because he just collected the old aluminum cans from the trash bins. He had this old broom handle that he balanced over his shoulder and from each end hung two shopping bags. Every bag was filled with cans that he scavenged from trash bins and garbage cans.

"Morning," I said.

Over his blue coveralls he wore a tweed coat that was perhaps a size too big for him, and I wondered if he'd found that in a trash bin too. "Good morning," he murmured, and walked on with a slow, steady shuffling gait.

I kept pace with him. "Say, is this a whole morning's work?" I pointed to the full bags.

"It's just part of it," he grunted. "I still have most of my route to do." He winked. "And then it's time to start over again in the afternoon."

I just stopped and stood still, watching him leave school. It's strange, but I'd never realized how many cans we threw away on campus. Imagine how much more aluminum just went to waste in the city—or even the state.

It really was a disposable society in a lot of ways. Throw things away and don't worry about them. Cans, cars, bottles—you name it and we junked it. Even people like Marsh.

I wanted to run after the other kids and shake some sense into them. But I played it cool and kept control of myself. I just wanted to find Howie.

As it turned out, the PE class involved some tumbling and light workouts on the rings and the horse. And that was good. I just let my brain wander off somewhere and let my body do my thinking for me. There was something clear and clean about working out on the rings and twisting my body this way and that in an easy, fluid motion.

When I was finished, Coach Lau came over. He was a small, lean man from Hawaii who'd been after me to join the gymnastics team. He'd said I was a natural, but I told him that I didn't go in for that school rah-rah business. I'd been a puzzle to him ever since then.

"I heard about Marsh. It's a tragic waste."

I shrugged, sorry that I didn't have time to savor the exercise; but I had to make an effort to talk to him. "Yeah. A real waste."

He fingered the whistle that hung by a cord around his

neck as if he was hunting for something else to say. "I'm glad to see that you came to school, though. Life has to go on after all."

"So I hear," I mumbled, and headed toward the next line of students waiting for a turn on the horse. Howie was there. Though he had size and muscle, he was short on coordination and had already almost dislocated his shoulder on the rings. As a result, he was eyeing the horse as if it were a new torture device.

"Just the man I wanted to see." I nudged Howie in the side.

Howie turned around, rubbing the spot where I had poked him. "Oh, Sean. Hey, too bad about Marsh. But I warned him about those brakes, you know?"

"Really," I said and paused a moment before I spoke again. It was hard to keep my voice calm and controlled. 'Say, just for curiosity's sake, could someone have done something to them to make it look like an accident?"

Howie stared at me real funny. So did the other kids who had overheard us. They twisted their heads around, and the look on their faces reminded me of a picture book I had when I was small. One page had shown a whole bunch of cows in a field when they had caught their first sight of a wolf. The cows' eyes had bulged out and their mouths were open—just like Howie and the others. I had blown it in my eagerness; but I was beyond the point of caring.

"Well, could someone?" I demanded.

"Are you crazy?" Howie shuffled along sideways toward the others as if seeking the protection of the herd.

I took another step toward him. "I want the truth, Howie."

"Okay, okay." He shoved his hands nervously at the air to make me stop where I was. "Sure, you could do things to the rear brakes. The line is only a thin metal pipe." He raised his thumbs and index fingers to illustrate. "So you can wriggle and bend it until it's just about to break." He spread out his hands. "And some day—you wouldn't know exactly when—the pipe would go."

"Could you tell if someone had tampered with it?" I asked intently.

From across the gym, Coach Lau blew his whistle. "No talking there."

Howie tried to use it as an excuse to turn around, but I wouldn't let him. "I need to know, Howie."

"Yes, there'd be evidence if they did," he shrugged. "The edges around the break ought to be bright and shiny."

I thought gloomily of the fire. "I doubt if there's much left of Marsh's car, let alone the rear brake line."

Howie backed up against the others. "Maybe you ought to talk to Ms. Semple?" he suggested nervously. Besides teaching English, she also acted as our class counselor.

That really got to me. "You're the one who has to talk to her. You're the one who needs the help." I pivoted so I could talk to them all. "Marsh is dead and yet none of you act like you really care. You just mouth phrases for a few minutes and then you act just the same as always."

"Come on, Sean." Howie folded his arms with a frown. "We're sorry that Marsh is dead, but we've got our own lives to lead."

I struggled to find the right words for my feelings. "That's almost like an excuse not to care."

Howie leaned forward. "Well, what do you want us to

do? Wear black armbands? Have a day of silence?" He gave a sniff. "Marsh was fun, but he could be a pain in the neck a lot of times."

"You're not sorry he's dead." I grabbed Howie by the T-shirt and shoved him backwards. And he was so off balance that his heels skidded and he fell, his back thudding against one of the mats spread over the gym's wooden floor.

When Howie got to his feet he had his fists raised, but someone grabbed his arm. "Hey, come on, Sean was in the car, remember?"

"Okay, okay." He opened his fists. "I guess you're right."

In the meantime, Coach Lau came striding over. A few feet away from us, he let the whistle drop from his lips so it dangled by the cord around his neck. "What's going on here?"

Howie shrugged and stared at me with lazy menace. "No problem, coach. I've got thirty pounds on Sean. He'd really have to be crazy to try something."

"Do you want to go home, Pierce?" the coach asked.

I looked around digustedly at the others. All of them lived in their nice, neat little fairy-tale world in the suburbs where the only real problems were acne and maybe sneaking into a R-rated movie. Murders were what happened in San Francisco, not in a nice little town like Almaden.

"Yeah, I think I'd better," I said.

Coach Lau walked me toward the door. "If I were you, Pierce, I'd try to forget about that accident."

"I wish I could," I said, and felt as if I were walking away from more than the gym, but from my whole little sheltered world.

7

On my way home from school, my usual route led right by Marsh's house, and I slowed my bike as I passed the driveway. Marsh's dad used to park his own car on the street, insisting that Marsh put his car on the driveway over an oil pan. The pan was still there with the residue of various oils from Marsh's car.

What if I could find fingerprints in the oil pan? Maybe one of them would belong to the murderer. At the very least, Lieutenant Silva and the others would have to take me seriously.

I got off my bike and walked up the gradual slope of the driveway to kneel beside the oil pan. Some dinosaur had given everything it had—just like the ads used to say—to provide the fluids for Marsh's Pinto. And though I saw a lot of interesting swirls and patterns, I didn't see one fingerprint.

"Mecca's that way," said a girl in a low, pleasant voice.

I looked up sheepishly to see Nora standing in the doorway of the Weisses' house and pointing to her right. She really wasn't all that bad-looking, in a comfortable sort of way. Everything about her was sensible, from her baggy coveralls to her blue turtleneck sweater. Even her brown hair had been cut into a short and practical helmet shape.

"Mecca?" I looked at her blankly.

She gave me a brittle smile. "That's the city that the Moslems face on their knees."

We had spoken a few times but it was mainly when she had been trying to get me to sign one of her many petitions. I hadn't known she was capable of making a joke.

I got to my feet, brushing off my knees. "Maybe I'm starting my own religion."

"Worshipping oil pans?"

I nudged the pan with my foot. "You can tell the future in them."

"Oh? And what do you see?"

"Profits on the rise for Standard Oil." I glanced down at the pan. "And Comet cleanser."

She stuffed her hands into her pockets. "Actually, I suppose we should get rid of it. It was always such an eyesore—but then Marsh's car always covered it up." She lowered her head and shuffled her feet together so that the wooden heels on her shoes made a *thok* sound. "We decided to hold the funeral on Saturday morning. It will be at the Evergreen Funeral Chapel."

"Did they have the autopsy?" I asked eagerly.

She stepped back, startled. "Why?"

I spread out my hands. "I've really got to know. I ... I...." For a moment my tongue kept running while my brain stopped. It seemed to take forever to connect the two back together again. "I keep thinking that I ran out on him."

"Oh, no." She shook her head quickly. "There was nothing you could have done. He died of a broken neck, before the fire."

It was such a relief to me that my shoulders sagged. "All this time I wasn't sure if I'd left him to die." Suddenly my eyes began to sting as if I was about to cry. Desperately I pinched the corners of my eyes to stop it, but the tears began to slip around my fingers and fall wet and hot down my cheeks. "I'm sorry," I said in embarassment. "I don't know what's gotten into me. I mean, I didn't even cry when my mom and dad broke up."

"Hey,"—she touched my elbow lightly—"it's okay for people to cry—both men and women."

I lowered my hand and saw that Nora was crying too. And I began to think that maybe I had been wrong about her. Of all the people in this phony place, she was the only one who took life seriously enough to miss Marsh. It made me feel a whole lot better inside—like a Martian who finds out he isn't the only one stranded on this planet.

I thought to myself that maybe I had been wrong to put her down all this time as some weird killjoy. Behind all that seriousness might be a person who really cared about people. "I just couldn't take it at school anymore."

She pursed her lips and gave her head a little nod. "I know how you feel. I wasn't up to going to school either."

The words came rushing out of me. "I don't know. Everyone at school acts like they just want to forget Marsh." I thought again of the Can Man. "It's almost like everyone's so much disposable trash."

Nora leaned her head to one side as if she was intrigued by me. "You're not at all like Marsh described you."

I swept my sleeve clumsily across my eyes and I couldn't help asking, "What did he tell you?"

Nora started to smile through her tears—this time in an easier, more natural way that reminded me a little of Marsh's smile. "He used to call you a closet accountant: behind that flip manner of yours was the soul of a bookkeeper struggling to get out."

"You're not like Marsh said either." I eyed her with growing amusement. "He called you the resident grouch."

Nora had a nice, throaty laugh. I really liked the sound of it. "I guess Marsh was the last person to trust when it came to being accurate about people."

I found myself grinning for the first time in days. "Yeah, good old Marsh." I squared my shoulders. "Well, I'd better get inside before someone mistakes me for a water fountain." But I felt reluctant to leave now that I'd found a kindred soul.

I guess Nora felt the same way because she produced two Kleenexes from one of her numerous pockets and handed one to me. "I don't think it's good to cry alone. Not today." She wiped at her eyes. "Most people didn't know what a soft side he had. But I still remember my first day at school when this fourth grader started to pick on me and Marsh came along. The boy was a lot bigger but even so Marsh managed to beat him up. He said no one could pick on me but him."

"That sounds like Marsh all right." I used the Kleenex on my eyes. The tears were still there, heavy at the corners, and yet I felt I had them under control now. "I really miss him."

Nora glanced at the oil pan. "This is a funny place for reminiscing. What were you doing in our driveway anyway?"

I shifted my feet uncomfortably. "I was . . . just curious."

"Curious about what?" Nora had become polite but firm—as if I were never going to get away until I had answered all of her questions. She would make a good prosecuting attorney.

I could feel my cheeks begin to redden, recalling Howie's reaction when I had told him my story. "You'll just think I'm crazy."

"Hey,"—she tapped a finger against a spot just below her throat—"I lived with Marsh all these years, remember?"

Well, I thought to myself, if Nora could believe in all those different political and industrial conspiracies, maybe she'd believe in one involving her brother. "I was just seeing if anyone had done something to Marsh's car." Ready to stop at the first sign of skepticism, I quickly outlined what Dad and Howie had said. "So maybe it's not anyone's fault, really. It's just a prank that got out of hand."

Nora placed her feet together and studied her toes. "I suppose it's a possibility."

I stared at her blankly. "Then you think it may be true?"

She looked up suddenly. "I know just how much Marsh

could exasperate people. There were times when I could quite cheerfully have strangled him myself." She scratched the tip of her nose. "At any rate, let's say I don't disbelieve you."

I didn't know whether to laugh or cry at that moment. I should have known that Nora would side with an underdog like me, at least temporarily. "I didn't find anything in the pan, though."

Nora brushed her fingertips back and forth across her lips for a moment. "Let's see. How do they do it on the cop shows?" She closed her eyes for a moment as she tried to remember. "You've got to have the motive, the means and the ... the...." She tapped a fingertip against her right temple. "Oh, what is that word?"

"I think it's 'opportunity,' " I suggested.

"That's it." She snapped her fingers. "I'm glad we watch the same programs."

I gave her a puzzled look. "I thought those kinds of things would be too silly for a serious person like you."

"Some people like to knit sweaters for cats; others like to put safety pins through their ears. Everyone has a secret indulgence." She pantomimed shooting a pistol. "Mine happens to be whodunits. I'm just naturally snoopy, I guess."

"Well, Ms. Sherlock, who do you think 'done' it?"

Nora cupped her chin in her hand. "Who was the butt of Marsh's worst practical jokes?"

I shrugged. "Are we talking institutional vandalism or personal humiliation?"

She waved her hand in the air. "I think we should forget the institutional stuff like the cherry bombs down the toilets."

I was a bit surprised at that. "When did that happen?"

"In middle school. I think Dad was still deducting the cost of replacing the plumbing from Marsh's allowance." Nora folded her arms over her stomach.

"And I guess we can forget about the stink and smoke bombs." I frowned thoughtfully, remembering that day when Marsh and I had become friends. "Well, there are those kids from Peterson High. They might still want to get even for what Marsh did to their quarterback."

"Marsh said he recognized one of those kids as Petey. He used to live near here before his family moved to Sunnyvale." She pointed toward the northwest.

"Well, that's one," I said.

"And there's Angela Ryerson." Nora dipped her hands into her pockets. "Marsh ruined her birthday party last year by slipping Ex-Lax into the candy dish."

"Howie's just started to go out with her," I said excitedly. "Do you think she could have put him up to it?"

"Maybe." And between Nora and myself, we managed to come up with a half-dozen more people in just a few minutes. Finally I put a hand to my forehead. "Marsh was certainly a busy little boy, wasn't he? I think we'd better start making up a list."

Nora reached over and grabbed my wrist, turning it slightly so she could look at my watch. "We could be at that most of the day. I'd rather be trying to narrow it down."

"Do you mean it?" I asked stupidly.

"Marsh certainly had his faults," she said quietly. "But he didn't deserve to die." She set her chin stubbornly.

The relief I felt was the emotion someone would feel after having been locked up in a dark closet with the air getting all heavy and stuffy and suddenly having Nora open the door. "But where do we start?"

"I know where Petey is likely to be right now. He's turned into a regular video rat. I saw him all the time at the video arcade this summer when I had a job at the Sunnyvale Shopping Mall. His high school's only a few blocks away. I'll bet he goes there during his lunchtime." She began to walk up the driveway. "Let me get my coat and we'll go over."

"But why is he so important?" I followed her toward her house.

She paused in front of a bed of hyacinths. "He's one of those fringe kids—you know, the kind who hang around the different cliques. He never gets invited to do much. But he overhears a lot of stuff. He might have picked up some rumors."

"That still sounds like a longshot," I frowned.

She jerked her head at me. "You can stay at home and mope all day. But I don't recommend it. The grief will just eat away at you if you don't try to do something about it."

I don't know why I thought I had been the only one to miss Marsh. I should have realized his family would. "I'm glad you're in my corner," I said, and bowed her through her front door.

8

WE JUST MANAGED TO CATCH A BUS THAT GOT US TO THE Sunnyvale Shopping Mall at about twelve noon. There were a lot of Peterson High kids hanging around the mall, just as Nora had predicted.

The mall itself was one of those enclosed shopping centers so that it had the same even environment and temperature all year round. It was a big one, too, covering several square blocks if you included the two-story parking lots. And within the mall were all kinds of stores designed to liberate all that money from bored, middle-class pockets. The shops ranged from places that sold music boxes to see-through, edible underwear to personalized balloons.

But despite all the bright lights and colors, the mall reminded me of a jail cell. No matter how many pretty pictures a prisoner might put up on the walls of a jail cell, you know the concrete is still there. And all the kids had this bored kind of expression—as if they were just killing time. They reminded me of the way prisoners stand around in the exercise yard in a prison movie.

The video arcade was crowded with kids, mostly boys, but there were also quite a few businessmen in suits and ties getting their afternoon fix of video.

"That's the manager." Nora pointed toward a fat little man in a green T-shirt and an orange vest.

Next to the manager, lounging against the doorway, was a tall, skinny man with long, dirty blonde hair underneath a feathered cowboy hat a size too small for him. His jeans were tucked into a pair of old motorcycle boots. He wore an orange vest too.

The manager's eyes never seemed to stay still but kept on looking down the rows of video games. "The Chipmunk's using slugs," we heard him say.

The skinny man shoved himself away from the doorway in a poor man's imitation of a bored Clint Eastwood. Making his way through the crowd, he grabbed a kid in a Peterson High jacket and swung the kid around. I recognized him as the chubby human paperweight who'd been sitting on my chest after that short fight—the one Marsh had called Petey.

"Out." The skinny man kept his teeth partially clenched together as he snarled the word from one corner of his mouth.

"But I've still got three spaceships," Petey protested. He glanced helplessly toward the game, which was making a series of little beeps and whoops as if the fate of the galaxy depended on his getting back to the machine.

"Out"—the skinny man jerked a thumb toward the doorway—"while you can still use those hands."

"But I wasn't doing anything wrong," Petey insisted.

The skinny man jabbed an index finger at him. "Don't give me that. You were using slugs and you know it."

Petey stared at the skinny man's hat. "In case you haven't heard, the urban-cowboy look is out."

"Yeah? Well, funny thing about that. Because so are you." And the skinny man frog-marched Petey through the crowd toward the doorway. Some other kid scurried over to the abandoned game to get a free play.

The manager never took his eyes off the rest of his customers. He simply stepped to the side as the skinny man passed by.

With one final jerk of his arms, the skinny man tossed Petey out of the arcade. "And don't let me catch you cheating again."

Petey sprawled on his stomach. "Nazi," he shouted over his shoulder.

"I was a marine." The skinny man barely curled up his lip scornfully as he went back to supporting the doorway.

"I rest my case," Petey said.

Nora walked over and peered down at him. "Hello, Petey."

He rolled over onto his back. "Oh, hi, Nora. Did you decide to see how the other half lives?"

"No, I heard there was a boy who flew through the air so I came to see for myself." Nora held out a hand to him. "Are you all right?"

"Sure." Petey took her hand and bounced to his feet. "It's a game we play every day. I slip a slug in every now and then and those goons try and catch me doing it."

"You ought to make a video game out of it," Nora suggested.

"Yeah, like Pac-Man." Petey began to dust off his clothes.

The more I looked at Petey, the more he reminded me of that funny chipmunk in the Disney cartoons—the one with the big nose. Underneath his jacket, he wore a light-blue polyester shirt that didn't quite cover his round little belly and his wide hips were encased in a pair of tight designer jeans.

He gave a laugh. "Harv's a little off today. He only threw me four feet."

"And they let you back in there?" Nora wondered.

"Sure"—the kid cocked his head to one side—"because in between slugs, I pour a lot of real tokens into their machines bought with real money. Besides, if Harv didn't have me to throw around, he'd have to go out and buy a set of real weights."

"Instead of one dumbbell?" In mock panic, Nora clapped her hand over her mouth. "Oops. Forget I said that."

But Petey only laughed. Apparently he was used to Nora's ways. "So what's up?"

Nora glanced at me. Apparently he hadn't heard about Marsh yet. She indicated me. "Did you meet my friend, Sean?"

He held up his hand and seemed to polish an invisible surface. "Hi." He paused and then squinted at me. "Do I know you?"

"I think you were sitting on my chest the last time we met."

"Oh, yeah." He wagged his finger at me. "You were the clown who got himself in trouble with Marsh."

I couldn't help wincing because I hadn't thought I'd made that much of a fool of myself. "Funny that you never tried anything again."

He spread out his hands wide and then clapped them against his sides. "Hey, if we'd lost the football game, we might've. But since we creamed you guys, we figured you'd taken enough punishment." He shook his head as he savored the memory of that game. "Thirty-seven to three."

"Come on, Petey," Nora coaxed him. "Somebody must have had a grudge."

Petey turned, looking suspiciously from Nora to me and back to her again. "Why? What happened?"

"Marsh . . . had an accident," Nora said carefully. I suppose she didn't want to frighten Petey by telling him about the final result.

Petey tapped his fingers indignantly against his chest. "And you think I had something to do with it?"

"Hey, don't hulk out on us." I tried to keep my voice as calm and soothing as I could. "We just thought you might have heard some rumors about somebody who did. It might not have been anything deliberate."

"I haven't heard anything." Petey crossed his arms back and forth several times in front of himself.

"You're sure?" I asked.

"Just how serious was Marsh's accident?" he demanded.

"Pretty bad," I said.

"Like how bad?" He jerked his head at Nora.

"Like dead," Nora said in a little voice.

Petey looked both shocked and hurt at the accusation. I felt almost as bad as if I had just accused Bambi of arson. "And you think I might have had something to do with it?"

"No, no," Nora was quick to reassure him, "it's just that you get around a lot. We thought you might have picked up some kind of rumors. You know, how someone might have wanted to get even with Marsh."

"I swear I haven't." Petey shook his head solemnly. "But if I do, you'll be the first to hear."

He sounded perfectly sincere to me, and apparently Nora thought the same way because she nodded her thanks to him. "Okay, Petey, I'd appreciate it."

But as she started to head for the nearest exit, Petey called to her. "Hey, Nora."

"Yes?" Nora turned around.

"I'm sorry to hear about Marsh," Petey said. "He certainly made life interesting."

"That he did," I agreed.

When we were outside the shopping mall, I jammed my hands into my pockets. "Well, what about Petey? Do you think he was telling the truth?"

Nora exhaled slowly. "Petey may be slightly dishonest, but he's not a liar. Lying takes too much work, and Petey is basically a lazy person. If he says he doesn't know anything, then I believe him."

"And you think he'll tell us about any gossip he hears?" I asked.

"He'll keep his promise," Nora said confidently.

"So we've put out feelers in Sunnyvale. Who do we

tackle next, Ms. Sherlock?" I was inclined to let Nora take the lead.

Nora tapped a finger against her lips, "Elementary, Watson. We go for the person with the best motive and the most know-how. Someone like Howie."

I thought of the run-in we'd had in the gym. "Well, I think you'll have to tackle him on your own. We're not exactly friends at the moment."

She drew her head back and frowned. "Howie could have been the brawn that caused the accident, but we need to find the one who gave him the push, so to speak. So we have to talk to Angela."

I tried to picture Angela in my head. But I could only remember a kind of fluffy blonde. "She's a sophomore, isn't she?" Nora made a face. "Yeah, she's one of these girls with teased hair and bubble gum for brains. She's been carrying around the same romance novel for months. I don't think she's gotten past page twenty."

"Maybe she's waiting for the Cliff Notes," I suggested.

Nora sniffed. "She'd need Cliff Notes for the Cliff Notes." She sat down on the bench to wait for the bus. "But how do we pry her loose from Howie so we can work on her?"

"That's easy," I said, sitting down beside her. "Howie's always complaining that he's stuck in seventh period while she's free to flirt over at the 7-Eleven."

It took a half hour for the bus to come and another hour for it to get us back to Almaden. And by the time we got back to Nora's house and grabbed a quick bite to eat, it was time to go looking for Angela; so we bicycled up to the 7-Eleven parking lot across the street from the school.

She was right where Howie had said she would be, on

the sidewalk to the side of the 7-Eleven. There were about a dozen kids with her and they were busy shouting at one another over the music booming from a portable stereo—until they saw us wheel into the lot. They just shut up and stared at me. I suppose most of the school had heard about that incident between Howie and me. By now, everyone probably thought of me as Sean Pierce, the wild boy of Borneo.

In fact, Angela jumped to her feet as if she were getting ready to hide inside the 7-Eleven.

"Hey, Angela," I called to her. "Tell Howie I'm sorry about this morning. I just kind of lost control of myself." I coasted up to the sidewalk and stopped with a bump. "I've been upset about the accident." I heard Nora stop about a yard away.

Angela pulled at the hem of her sweater and she trotted out what seemed to be an all-purpose word. "Really." Her voice dropped a little on the last syllable to indicate sympathy. She reached over and patted Nora on the arm.

"Yeah," another kid said, "I was sorry to hear about Marsh too. It must have been awful."

I almost blurted out how terrible it was, but I took a lesson from that morning and managed to keep control of myself. "It was. But I've got to learn to live with it."

Angela seemed to relax a little. "Really?"

Those detectives on the TV shows always know what to say when they're interrogating a suspect—but then they have scriptwriters putting words into their mouths. And while I couldn't think of what to say, I thought that my tone ought to be sincere. And the most sincere person I could think of was Robert Young in that doctor show and all those Sanka commercials.

"It's too bad Marsh got killed. I know he was starting to

feel bad about some of the tricks he'd pulled." It was a lie, but I remember some history teacher telling us that the most effective lies were the big ones—especially when people wanted to believe them.

"Re-e-eally." Angela looked as skeptical as the others.

"People change," I shrugged. "They grow up."

Angela stroked one of her elbows. "Really," she murmured under her breath.

"He didn't mean to hurt people's feelings. He just didn't think," I went on quickly. "But he was beginning to realize what he'd done. It's a shame he didn't get to apologize to some of his victims."

Angela thought that over for a moment and sighed in agreement. "Really."

My fingers tightened around the handlebars as I figured out what I ought to say next. "I mean, people might not hate him so much now." And I held my breath as I watched Angela for some guilty reaction.

But she only looked at me puzzled. "Not really?"

"Come on," I coaxed her, "you must have heard how some of the other kids have been bad-mouthing Marsh."

She shook her head, looking surprised at the news. "Not really."

I studied her but I didn't think she was pretending. Even if Angela had the inclination to lie, I don't think she had the brains for it. I glanced at Nora to see if she had anything else to ask, but she had this pained look on her face as if she were sitting on a tack. And since she didn't seem to want to talk, it made it hard to figure out what was wrong.

Anyway, my first priority was to get out of there. "Well, that's all." I turned my front wheel so I could roll away. "I just wanted to tell you that."

Angela waved at me a bit more brightly now. "It's been nice."

Nora frowned at me as we bicycled back onto the street. "You lied."

"But I think I found out what we wanted to know," I shrugged indifferently. "And anyway, what's the diff if I told a lie? It made some people think better of Marsh."

My first reaction was to tell her to stop being to stiff-necked and high-minded, but I checked my angry words. It seemed important to keep hold of the one person in Almaden who had some faith in me.

"Things always seem to work out better when you tell the truth." She lifted one hand from the handlebar of her bike and touched my arm.

I had my doubts about that, but if I'd said so, Nora might have wanted some kind of explanation. And I didn't feel up to it. Not now. "Okay, I'll try it your way for a while."

Satisfied, she put her hand back on her handlebar. "I think we can write Angela off the list, don't you?"

"Really," I mimicked Angela.

Nora stretched one arm out and swung it in a lazy circle. "I don't know about you, but I feel better now that I'm actually doing something."

I was dropping behind so I pumped at the pedal. "It's a lot better than staying at home and moping."

Nora slowed and angled in near the pavement as a low-rider cruised on by. "Do you feel up to school tomorrow?"

I almost panicked at the thought of having to face Howie and Coach Lau and the other kids.

"Do you?" I asked her.

She coasted along on her bike for a few yards. "Not

really. But I have to know if someone accidentally killed him."

I certainly had to admire her spirit. "I need to know too. For my own sake, if not for Marsh's."

"But the honest way," she warned me.

"I'll be a regular boy scout." I held up my right hand.

"I was hoping you'd say that." And she flashed one of those patented Weiss smiles at me.

9

It wasn't easy going back to school, but I would have felt worse staying at home and leaving Nora to do all the dirty work. So I went along with her. I stayed calm by reminding myself that I was doing something about Marsh's death.

I can't say, though, that we had much luck. Nora would tell our suspect that she was sorry if that person hated Marsh for what he'd done. And of course, they would deny it hotly and honestly—or so it seemed.

By the end of two days, we'd gone through our first list

of suspects and were compiling a second list at Nora's house when I finally shook my head in discouragement.

"Nora, look how long this list is already."

Nora studied the list of twenty names. "There aren't so many people here."

I threw my pencil on top of the coffee table in disgust. "But that only includes the people Marsh tricked this year!"

Nora tucked her feet behind the front legs of her chair and sagged backwards wearily. "If we started with kindergarten and worked our way up to eleventh grade, we'd probably have to list a third of the kids who went to school with Marsh."

"Yeah." I fingered the list regretfully. "And even if you could rule out the kids, Marsh has played a lot of jokes outside school."

Nora placed one hand against her cheek and gave me a tired smile. "I remember the time he wound a bicycle chain around the front doors to the library. People had to use the rear doors until the fire department could cut the chain."

"Really?" I drew my eyebrows together. "He didn't tell me that. I'm surprised that they let Marsh back into the library."

Nora planted her feet on the floor. "It was years ago."

"Well, he didn't reform much then. We were there just a couple of weeks ago," I said. "We had this punishment assignment and we wound up going there." I couldn't help adding, "Marsh let the air out of the tires on a Porsche. We thought it was Ms. Semple's car, but it belonged to this bald-headed guy instead." I scratched my throat. "The funny thing is that I was sure he wrote down the number on Marsh's license plate. Only he never came by to complain." I hesitated, though, about describing the guy's radar eyes. I was positive she would laugh at me the way Marsh had.

But instead, she bit her lip thoughtfully. "Was that Porsche a gold one?"

I felt a kind of electric shock, like someone had touched me with a cattle prod. "Yeah. Did Marsh talk about it?"

"No, but I saw one parked outside late one night just before the accident." She pointed in the direction of the street. "It's funny, but it had this corny decal on the trunk."

"A flower?"

Nora nodded her head sharply. "Do you think it's a coincidence?"

I got up and looked through her living-room window toward the street. "That driver had a real strange look on his face—like he was going to get even." I turned away in frustration. "But how are we going to find just one gold Porsche in the whole Bay Area?"

Nora crossed the room to the little stand where their telephone sat. "My uncle has a Porsche and he's always complaining about all the tune-ups it needs. A Porsche is like a fine watch that has to be kept just right. We can call around the agencies that would do maintenance work."

She was starting to open the phone book, but I covered the pages with my hand. "Nora, I've tried things your way. Now let me try it mine."

"I'm not sure . . ." she began.

"Please, Nora," I pleaded, "this is our best lead so far."

"What are you going to say?" she demanded suspiciously.

"It'll be just a little white lie," I promised.

She shoved my hand away. "Well, I reserve the right to

censor your story if I think your little white lie is changing color."

When I called the first Porsche agency, I improvised this whole line about how this bald-headed customer had left his umbrella in the store where I worked. "I saw him drive off in a gold Porsche with a flower decal on the back. I tried to call to him, but he was too far away."

I struck out with them, but Nora gave her grudging approval. "Well, you're bending the truth a bit more than I like, but I guess I can live with it."

So, with Nora's blessing, I began to work my way down the list alphabetically though I didn't have much luck until I got the Sunnyvale Porsche Agency. They knew a Ms. Semple had a Porsche, but it turned out that her husband had a full head of hair.

While I was calling Sunnyvale, Nora occupied herself by writing down the remaining three phone numbers on a note pad. "This next one's in Almaden." She tapped her finger by the number. "The Sebesta Porsche Agency." She tore off the page and handed it to me. "And after this we can try the foreign-car repair shops."

"There are a dozen of those." I stared at the telephone book. "The phone's going to be molded to my ear."

"It'll look good on you," she said as she began to put more numbers down on the pad.

I was just going to suggest taking a break after this phone call when someone answered at the other end of the line. "Hello?" I asked in my pleasantest voice. "I'm trying to return something to the owner of a gold Porsche." It took a moment for the agency receptionist to connect me with a salesman and then I went into my spiel. "So I was wondering if you'd know the owner. He'd be a bald-headed man."

"Yes," the salesman said in a slow, deliberate voice, "we do have a client who might fit your description. He certainly drives a car like that."

I pressed the tip of my index finger against my thumb so Nora could see. "Oh? And what's his name?" Nora eagerly held her pencil poised over the pad.

"Russ Towers," the salesman said. "He's in the Almaden phone book, I believe."

"Russ Towers," I repeated slowly so Nora could write it down. "Thank you."

When I had hung up the phone, she winked at me. "Not bad for our second day in the detective business."

"I'll tell the FBI to get two desks ready for us." I began to thumb through the Almaden directory.

She craned her neck toward me curiously. "What're you doing?"

"The salesman said Russ might be in the phone book. I suppose it makes sense. He'd probably drop his car off at the agency closest to his house." In my impatience, the pages seemed stuck together.

"Here, let me do that." Nora turned the pages efficiently through the white section until we found Russ Towers. There were two entries under that name, in fact. One was for Joyel Electronics at an address in the heart of Silicon Valley. The other was a house address only a mile away.

I scratched the tip of my nose. "What do you know. He's a neighbor. Funny that my dad never visited him."

"Your dad knows Russ?" Nora played with the telephone cord.

"I never met him, but Dad used to work with him." I shut the phone directory. "Actually, you can't meet my dad without knowing about Russ. It's his favorite story."

Sixteen years ago, Russ had wanted Dad to quit the

company that employed both of them and start their own little outfit on the money they could borrow on their houses and cars. To Dad's great regret, he'd refused, and Russ had gone on to found Joyel Electronics, now one of the biggest in the area.

Nora nodded her head when I finished telling her what I knew about Russ. "So what do you think? Could it be Russ?"

I shrugged. "I don't know much more about Russ than what I already told you." I'd always cut Dad off before he could babble about Russ for very long.

Nora picked up the telephone receiver. "Well, it doesn't sound like a company president would be pulling a prank like that. Why don't you keep on calling?"

But when calls to the other agencies didn't turn up any more suspects, it looked like we were stuck with Ross Towers after all.

"Well," I sighed, "let me see what I can find out from Dad when he comes home for dinner."

Dad's company had staggered hours so he had to be at work by seven-thirty in the morning. But he got off at around four. After jogging at the park, he got home by five.

When Dad arrived, he had to park in our driveway because the garage was filled with movers' boxes that we still hadn't unpacked. I had the door open for him as he trudged along the little concrete path, a bucket of chicken under one arm and a dripping sack in the other.

"Hi, Dad. Let me give you a hand." I took the bucket from him.

"Yeah. Good." He put the palm of his free hand underneath the sack. "The kids at that stupid chicken place didn't put the lid on tight enough over the gravy."

"We don't use it anyway." I backed away from the door so Dad could step in.

"But it comes with the chicken," Dad said stubbornly. He held the sack carefully in front of him as he put it in the sink. "It won't take more than a few seconds to clean up the driveway."

I tried to keep myself from getting annoyed with him as I set the bucket down on the table. "Couldn't it wait until after dinner, Dad?"

"I don't want to draw any ants." Dad was already out the door again. He was a real nut about doing things neat and orderly. It's just too bad that his family didn't perform as well as one of his computers.

I set the table and then took the cole slaw from the soggy sack and got out butter and jelly from the refrigerator for the buns that were still inside the bucket. I even had the coffee warmed up by the time Dad had come back in from hosing off the driveway and path. "What a mess." He rubbed at a spot he'd found on his jogging jacket.

"I think you're supposed to presoak something like that." I lifted the lid from the bucket as the steam rose upwards. "But I'll ask Mom when I call her this week."

Dad sat down, ignoring the grease stain. "You'll do no such thing. Do you want her to think that we can't manage without her?" He grabbed the first piece of meat he could from the bucket and began chomping away.

"That's dark meat," I said.

He looked down, surprised. "So it is." I took a piece of white meat from the bucket and offered it to him. "I thought you hated dark meat."

He began chewing more deliberately. "It's my dinner and my jacket."

I shrugged and began to eat my chicken. "It's your right to ruin both if you want."

Dad dumped the chicken down on his plate. "This is going all wrong, sport. Let's start over." He forced himself to smile. "So how did your day go?"

I opened up the container of cole slaw. "I tried to go to school today, but I left."

Dad took another piece of chicken from the bucket and inspected it carefully before he began eating. "I guess settling back into a normal routine isn't going to be easy for you."

It was the closest he had ever come to seeing my point of view. Usually my workaholic father was too caught up in his own projects.

"It's not so bad in some ways." I spooned cole slaw onto my plate.

Dad nodded his thanks when I spooned some onto his plate. "I knew you'd get to like Almaden after a while."

I slit open a bun and buttered it while it was still warm. Today was one of those rare days when Dad wanted to chat so I asked the million-dollar question. "Doesn't Russ Towers live around here?"

"As a matter of fact, he does. But what makes you so interested in Silicon Valley? You never were before." He thrust a forkful of cole slaw into his mouth.

"It's . . . it's a homework project." I edged forward on my seat. "We're studying the history of local companies."

Dad set down his fork and stared at his plate as if he'd suddenly lost his appetite. "Well, I wish I'd known how successful Russ was going to be." He smiled crookedly. "There are probably only a few hundred people who can come up with a product and start selling it. But there's only a handful who can handle the company when it grows large. And it's even harder to keep control of it."

Puzzled, I frowned at Dad. "It doesn't sound as if you like Russ."

"*Like* is maybe the wrong word for him." And from what Dad went on to tell me, Russ sounded like one mean corporate infighter. Someone who liked to get in close and then pound the daylights out of an opponent with quick, hard blows.

I wiped the grease from my fingers on a paper napkin. "He's really that tough?"

Dad settled back in his chair. "Once Russ sets his mind on something, nothing stops him. Even when his wife and daughter died, I hear he was right at work the next morning."

I crumpled up my napkin into a ball. "How did they die?"

Dad brushed his napkin across his mouth. "They were killed in a car crash about seven years ago. It would have broken most people to have something like that happen."

I started to clear away the plates. "So no one messes with Russ?"

Dad put the lid back on the bucket. "He's a mean one to tangle with. I hear he keeps a whole law firm busy suing people."

I set the things down before I dropped them. "So you wouldn't cross him?"

Dad gave a grunt. "I'd sooner stick my hand down a tiger's throat."

10

NORA JUST TOOK OVER AFTER THAT. SHE VERY CALMLY informed me that the two of us were going to check the back issues of the newspapers in the library. I don't think I would have gone there if the suggestion hadn't come from her. I didn't enjoy the idea of going back to the spot because of all the associations it brought. But I was really getting to like Nora. She was smart and she was tough and I wouldn't have traded her help for a whole army of lawyers.

And anyway, I don't think I had much choice. Arguing

with Nora was like trying to argue with a steamroller.

It wasn't easy riding our bikes to the library, even though we used side streets. During rush hour, all those white-collar types in their big cars are eager to get home so they seem to blame you for getting in their way, even when you're using a bike lane or a crosswalk.

I felt really funny when we got to the library. The parking spaces had different cars there, of course, under a bright, clear sky that always seems so startling in Almaden whenever the winds get rid of the usual layer of smog. The parking lot looked so innocent that it didn't seem like the kind of place where a murder could have started.

Nora knew exactly what to do, filling out the slips of paper to get the spools of microfilm on which the newspapers had been recorded. I suppose she knew all that stuff from researching all her political causes.

When she had the spools, she guided me over to two machines with rectangular screens. "Know how to use one of these?" she asked.

I stared at it without enthusiasm. "No, I've always sworn by TV myself."

She sat me down in front of one of them, switched the reader on and fed the microfilm underneath the lens onto the take-up spool. And then, very efficiently, she showed me how to use it.

I started with newspapers from seven and a half years ago while Nora took the next six-month period. It was kind of boring turning a crank and watching the newspapers slip by. It's funny, though, how the news doesn't change all that much—there always seem to be murders, riots and wars happening some place in the world. "Do you read through these old microfilms all the time?" I asked her.

She went on scanning the headlines intently while she spoke. "You have to have accurate information if you're going to criticize intelligently."

"Don't you ever get depressed?" I found myself looking at the want ads so I purposely began to crank faster to skip the microfilm to the next day. "Nothing ever seems to change. The world seems to be stuck with the same old messes."

"The more things change, the more they remain the same," Nora muttered. "That's a paraphrase of the French."

"Well, what's the use, whether we're talking English or otherwise?" I fiddled with the crank.

"Because someone has to begin to take a stand," she said calmly enough. "And eventually maybe other people will join you."

We had been reading headlines for about another hour when Nora murmured, "Bingo." I leaned over to look at her screen and read:

> The wife and daughter of prominent businessman Russell Towers died today in a tragic car crash. Elaine Towers, 38, and her daughter, Joy, 10, were driving north along San Tomas Expressway when a car driven by Ray Ballano, 18, swerved over the divider into their lane.

I paused for a moment. Elaine and Joy. Joy and Elaine. Joyel. I hadn't given it much thought since there are so many companies with funny names in Silicon Valley. But it was obvious now where he'd gotten the name for his business.

"He must have thought a lot of his family if he named

the company after them," I said to Nora.

"But what happened to the kid?" she wondered.

I was curious too, so we kept on reading until I found a little article buried on the back page of a newspaper dated a month later. The boy had his license suspended for drunk driving and was put on three years' probation.

Nora let out a soft whistle as she read over my shoulder. "That kid must have had some lawyer."

I tapped the screen. "If you don't think you can work it out with the parents and you don't trust the police, but you're still the kind of person who believes in getting even, then you just might decide to do things yourself."

Nora sat back down before her machine. "Let's see if the kid met with any 'accidents'?"

It was fifteen minutes before closing time when one of the library clerks came over to tell us we had to turn in our microfilms. I slumped at my chair. "And we haven't even gone through a year's worth of newspapers. This could take forever."

Nora began to rewind the microfilm. "And for all we know Ballano's family may have moved away from here after his probation."

I wound my own machine's crank furiously. "Or we could have missed it. Marsh only got a few lines in the obituaries."

Nora put her microfilm spool into its box. "Maybe it's time to take more direct action."

"Like what?" The microfilm came off the take-up spool with a loud crack.

Nora began to stack the microfilm boxes in front of her. "I think we ought to visit Russ's house. Maybe his car will be in the driveway."

I swallowed. "You mean go there?"

She glanced at me. "We don't have to go up and ring his doorbell, if that's what you're afraid of. But we ought to see if we both recognize the car."

"Yeah, I guess." I snapped off the reader unhappily. It seemed to me that we might be jumping right into a snake pit.

The houses in Russ's neighborhood were maybe ten or fifteen years old, which made them almost ancient by Almaden's standards. The streets were named after trees and plants and didn't run in straight lines but curved with odd twists and turns like a maze.

Russ's house didn't look any different from the others on that street. In fact, it looked almost like the model homes that some developer keeps to show the buyers how good a house can look. I mean the lawn hadn't just been mowed, it looked like it had been trimmed with scissors and a ruler—as if the grass were doing its best to imitate Astroturf. The house itself looked newly painted and the windows were bright and clean.

"Are you sure that's the place?" Nora asked.

"That's the address in the phone book." Russ's car wasn't in sight; and somehow, just looking at the house in the light of the streetlamps made all our ideas seem wild and absurd. "It doesn't look like the home of a crazed killer, does it?"

"No," Nora said. She had a stubborn look on her face. "But I still want to see that car and make sure."

"Tomorrow, after school then?" I asked.

She nodded her head once. "You've got a date."

It was kind of strange when we went there after school the next day. Though it was daytime, there weren't any other kids around. It was kind of spooky, like one of those *Twilight Zone* episodes where a person wakes up and is the only one left in the world.

But this time there was a gold Porsche parked in front of the garage. We coasted by slowly and I saw the faded daisy sticker on the trunk.

"That's it," I hissed to Nora. My legs felt almost numb, and suddenly it was hard to pedal. I tried to keep going—wanted to keep going, in fact. But it was as if my mind and body had gone out of sync. I wobbled on for about another fifty yards before I nearly fell off my bike. Finally, I just stopped and tried to calm down.

"Are you okay?" Nora stopped beside me.

"I will be in a moment. How do the Hardy Boys and Nancy Drew always manage to stay so cool?" I had to fight to take deep, even breaths.

"They must have been at it for something like fifty years." But Nora looked pretty pale. "I think it's the car I saw too. I don't think too many Porsches have decals like that."

I frowned at the Porsche. "Why do you think Russ has one on his car?"

"Maybe Joy put it on there." Nora shrugged. "Who knows?"

At that moment, a kid of about twelve swung his bike around the corner. Strapped over the handlebars was a large bag full of rolled-up newspapers. He pedaled slowly, having trouble turning his bike because of his load.

As he rode along, he tossed a newspaper onto the driveway of the house to the left. It hit the concrete and skidded into the rosebushes. The next paper landed straight on a lawn where a sprinkler quickly soaked it. But when he reached Russ's house, he stopped the bike and swung his legs off. Then, tugging a newspaper out of the bag, he walked up the driveway and placed the newspaper carefully against the front door.

My hand tightened around the handlebars of my bike. "Now that's something you don't see every day."

"Yes, and I don't think he's doing it because he wants to be the newsboy of the month." Nora got off her bike and propped it up. "Hey, wait a moment, will you?"

The carrier looked up when she called but went on walking briskly to his bicycle as if the last thing he wanted to do was to be caught on Russ's property. "You want a newspaper?"

Nora stood beside his bike. "No, we subscribe to the morning newspaper."

"I got a spare." The boy straddled his bike.

I finally got the message. Leaving my bike, I crossed the street. "All I've got is three dimes," I said as I dug my hand around in my pocket.

"That'll do." He snatched the coins from my outstretched palm and jerked out a newspaper.

I took it from the little pirate. "The paper only costs a quarter."

"So next time carry the right change." He stowed the dimes away. "I'm like a vending machine. You don't get change from them either."

I tucked the newspaper underneath one arm. "Let me know when you start your own company, will you? I want to be the first in line to buy stock."

He started walking his bike along the sidewalk. "So what do you want?"

We kept pace with him: Nora was on his left; I was on his right. "Do you know the man who lives back there?" She pointed toward Russ's house.

The boy glanced quickly over his shoulder as if he was afraid that Russ might appear any second. The look told me a lot already. "Stay clear of the guy. He's got it in for kids."

"Like what?" Nora asked eagerly.

The boy looped a newspaper high over her head onto the roof of a garage. "Like he's always staring at you if you walk across his lawn."

"Oh," Nora said in a disappointed voice. "Is that why you give him special treatment."

"Naw." He swung another newspaper onto a lawn with a sharp flick of his wrist. "Frankly, I think he's just a pain. The only time anyone sees him is when he comes to complain about what some kid's done."

A new thought struck me. "Especially boys? Teenage boys?"

The kid kept pushing himself along on his bike. "Well, I did hear about him hassling the Boyer twins." The kid nodded his head toward the house that was directly to our left. "He complained about their stereo. They used to crank it up so they could hear it while they were working on their car. It was an old 50s Chevy, so it always needed some repair."

"Then they were outside most of the time?" Nora asked.

"Yeah." He readied a new paper in his hand. "But their dad told Russ to buzz off because it was a public street." He launched the paper into the air. "They always figured it was Russ who wrecked the car but they never had any proof."

The three of us watched the paper land right in the center of a large shrub. "What happened to their car?" Nora asked.

The kid lowered his voice as if he didn't want anyone to overhear. "They were backing it out one day when the brakes went. It rolled across the street into their neighbor's garage door."

I grabbed his bicycle and forced him to stop so suddenly that he almost went headfirst over the handlebars. "Did they ever tell the cops?"

Maybe I was just a little too eager because the kid leaned back. "Why should they? It was an old car. I mean the taillights didn't even work on the thing. The cops gave them so many tickets that their dad eventually made them sell it for scrap."

Nora looked back at the house the kid had pointed out to us. "Do you know if the Boyers are home?"

The boy jerked his bicycle out of my hands. "No, the family moved about six months ago."

Nora rubbed a thumb across her forehead. "Well, do you know where they went?"

"People are always moving in and out in this neighborhood. Who keeps track?" The boy narrowed his eyes suspiciously.

I stuffed my hands into my pockets. "We think he wrecked the car of a friend of mine."

"Yeah?" The kid looked first at Nora and then at me, as if he had just seen some kind of brand on our foreheads marking us for the slaughter. "That's tough luck."

Nora took his arm. "If you tell the cops about Russ's reputation, maybe they'll investigate."

"And what if an accident happens to me? I only live two blocks away from him." He pulled free from Nora's grip.

We heard a door open suddenly and the three of us turned almost at the same time to look. A tall, bald-headed man stepped out of Russ's house and picked up his newspaper. As he straightened up, he saw us. He froze instantly.

"Oh-oh," the kid whispered.

"He doesn't know what we've been talking about," I told him.

The kid pushed down on the pedals and started rolling away from us. "I don't think I should even be within a block of you."

"Hey, wait." I snatched at his shoulder, but he was just out of reach.

"We've got to fight him together," Nora called.

But the kid just kept pedaling faster and faster, without throwing any newspapers.

"So much for the future hopes of this world." I turned. Russ was still staring at us. I threw the newspaper into the gutter. "Well, he knows we're onto him. What do we do now?"

Nora stared back at him defiantly. I had to hand it to her. She wasn't about to back down in front of anyone. "I think," she said out of the side of her mouth, "that it's time for us to go to the police."

I tugged at my ear uneasily, aware of Russ's watchful eyes. "We don't have much."

"We've already done part of their job for them. It's time they did the rest—unless you want to handle Russ all by yourself." Then, as if she wasn't afraid of her brother's murderer at all, Nora deliberately turned her back on Russ and strode over toward her bike.

I closed my eyes for a moment and told myself to stay calm. Facing Russ had to be worse than facing the Almaden cops. What happened in Belmont had to be ancient history by now. Even so, as I trailed Nora to our bikes, I felt like someone who had two fun choices: being eaten by a shark or being eaten by piranhas.

As we started to bicycle away, I couldn't help looking over my shoulder. Russ was still there, watching our every move with those radar eyes of his.

11

Lieutenant Silva was sitting before a computer monitor in an office. "So what can I do for you?"

"This is Nora Weiss," I said."Marsh's sister."

"How do you do, Ms. Weiss. I met your parents the other day." He typed something on the keyboard in front of him. "What can I do for you?"

"We've got some evidence that might indicate the car crash was more than an accident," Nora said, and nudged me.

My face reddening, I told the lieutenant about the tire

prank. With a frown, he turned from the monitor to consult a computer handbook. "I suppose you thought you were helping the owner?"

"All right," I admitted, "so we were out of line, but I'm serious about the rest."

"Did the owner threaten you in any way?" The lieutenant began retyping the instruction.

"Not exactly." My fingers polished the top of the filing cabinet beside me.

"Let me handle this." Nora stepped up next to me, and I was glad to turn things over to her. "But the owner's this character who likes to get even. The neighborhood kids are all scared of him."

"What's he done? Played Lawrence Welk too loud?" There was the faintest scornful curl to the lieutenant's mouth.

Nora folded her arms over her stomach and regarded him coolly. "We heard a lot of worse things about Russ Towers."

The lieutenant's fingers paused over the keyboard for a moment. "What about him?"

Quickly she told the newsboy's story, but even as she began to tell him my theory about the prank that had gotten out of hand, the lieutenant began to type at the keyboard again, as if he was growing impatient with us.

"I could fill a warehouse with reports of people who don't like kids playing on their lawns or who complain about noise." His eyes stayed intently on the monitor. "And as for the Boyers' car—well, it wouldn't be the first rustbucket to have its brakes fail."

Nora, however, refused to give up. "But it could have been Russ." She ticked the reasons off on her fingers. "First, he likes to get even so that's his motive. Second, he had the opportunity." She pointed a finger at Lieutenant Silva like a pistol. "I saw his gold Porsche parked across the street late one night."

The lieutenant rolled his eyes toward heaven. "Save me from children who watch Perry Mason reruns." Then he gave her a thin, cold smile. "In case you haven't heard, it's legal to visit friends and park your car on the street."

Nora leaned an arm on top of the monitor. "But it all adds up. I mean, this drunken kid kills his wife and daughter. So maybe he's got this bug in his head against kids in cars now. If you just checked your files...."

The lieutenant held up a hand. "There's no need. I worked on the case." He shifted heavily in his chair. "Don't you think that poor guy's suffered enough?" Lieutenant Silva began typing at the keys again.

It was just the right sort of thing to make Nora hesitate. But not me. "It's worth investigating at least. I bet something happened to that Ray Ballano."

The lieutenant sneered. "Maybe I'll begin checking after I finish learning all about Mr. Rosniak."

"Mr. Rosniak?" I straightened up, feeling as if someone had just run an ice cube down my spine. I hadn't ever expected to hear that name again.

"Contrary to what you seem to think, I haven't exactly been sitting around." He tapped one key and lines began to appear on the monitor and a printer began chattering off to one side. "After the accident, I did some investigating of my own—though you may not like what I turned up."

"Who's Mr. Rosniak?" Nora asked. But for a moment my brain was too numb to answer. "Who's Mr. Rosniak?" She demanded in a sharper voice.

I concentrated all my attention on the lieutenant, trying to keep him from saying too much. "That was over four years ago. I was just a kid."

The lines went on appearing on the monitor, sending a faint light flickering over the lieutenant's face. "And a pretty dumb one at that."

Nora was pulling at my arm to get me to face her, but I just couldn't. It's funny. You can live with someone for years and never really get to know them—like Dad. Or you can be with someone for just a day and feel like you've known them all your life. I was scared, really scared of losing Nora. Still hoping to keep him quiet, I spoke to the lieutenant instead. "I know. But I've paid for that little trouble...."

"Breaking and entering isn't just a little trouble," the lieutenant snapped. "Not when you steal stereos and TVs."

"It wasn't just me," I protested desperately. I tried to think of some other way to get him to shut up, but I couldn't come up with anything.

"That's true." He rose from his chair and went over to the printer. "According to you, it was a regular gang led by a certain Mr. Rosniak who just happened to talk all of you into stealing."

"We were just reading *Oliver Twist* in school," I said, trying to play it cool; but my insides were getting all cold and twisted up.

"Tsk, tsk. And they say kids don't learn anything useful in school nowadays." He tore a sheet out of the printer.

"Did you really steal?" Nora asked uncertainly.

I turned around finally to look at her; and it cut me up inside to see that the feistiness was gone now. And in its place was a doubting look that I didn't like.

"Did you?" Her voice had taken on a harder, more suspicious edge.

"You can't go by that."

And I started to tell her about that time four years ago—shortly after Mom had left Dad—when some friends and I had begun to steal stuff in Belmont.

It had all been pretty stupid. I mean, it wasn't like I really needed the money, even though Dad only gave me a dollar for mowing the lawn and was pretty stingy about paying for other chores too. Still, I could have managed. Mom always sent a check in her letters to me. And anyway the man—Rosniak wasn't his actual name—didn't pay us all that much when we did bring our loot to him. And we didn't do anything with the money except spend it on movies and video games. My friends and I stole more for the thrill of it.

There really wasn't much to do in Belmont except watch the lawns grow, so there had been a kind of excitement to stealing. At first, we had just picked houses where the front doors had been left unlocked. But after a while, watching a couple of useful TV crime shows, we had learned how to force windows open. We'd gotten to the point where we'd even stalk our prey, trying to find couples that worked during the day.

The guy deserved the charge of fencing stolen goods, but he hadn't deserved the charge of getting us to steal. It had been our idea, after all. Finally, one of us had worked up enough nerve to tell the truth. I'm ashamed to say that it wasn't me who was the first to speak up.

But after that, I was the one who got all the blame—not only for concocting the Fagin story but for coming up with the idea of stealing in the first place. Everyone figured that if I would lie about something like that, I was probably lying about all the rest.

Except for the brief reminder from Dad, I hadn't let myself think about Belmont. I thought it was because I had built up all these strong walls inside. But now the walls were starting to crumble and it felt like there was nothing I could do. It was like watching the ocean wash away a sand castle.

I held out my hand to her. "I didn't tell you about the thefts because we moved to get away from my past. I never even told Marsh."

Nora sucked in her breath indignantly. "Hiding the truth is as bad as lying."

"You let me lie to the car agencies," I pointed out.

"It's not in the same league," Nora said.

The lieutenant turned to Nora. "Perhaps I shouldn't be telling you this, but Sean was on probation himself for a year." He got up and went over to the printer. "Before his trial, the court appointed a psychiatrist to examine him." He cupped his hand over his chin while he scanned the printout. "It makes for some pretty interesting reading."

The words came out of me in a panicked rush. "The court psychiatrist was a jerk. I was just playing a game with him, you know? I wanted to see how much I could make him write down. I got him to fill up a whole notebook in just one session."

"The court psychiatrist seemed to think it was more than a game." The lieutenant tore the sheet from the printer. "It says here that he considered you a pathological liar."

"I was just a kid who made things even worse by being stupid," I said, feeling miserable and angry. "But I went to a regular shrink after that. Phone him. He'll tell you I'm not sick anymore. I don't even have to see him."

"You shouldn't say sick," Nora corrected me in a voice that was just a little too sweet and too kind.

I didn't like having Nora patronize me. It made my insides feel as brittle as glass. "You heard the newsboy. He told us about the Boyer twins."

Nora raised her shoulders and then let them drop. It was a small enough shrug. But it might just as well have been a guillotine blade falling on my neck. "So he has a bad reputation. There's nothing to prove that he tampered with Marsh's car."

I had lost Nora and it felt nearly as bad as when I had lost Marsh. "How can you feel sorry for your brother's murderer?"

Exasperated, the lieutenant said, "I don't know what kind of kicks you get by playing a joke like this, but I hope you didn't lose your regular psychiatrist's number."

I flattened my hand against my chest. "Now you're making me sound like some weird creep."

There was a long, terrible pause while I waited for Nora to make some sort of denial. What really hurt was the soft, pitying look she gave me. I could have taken angry words and insults and maybe even a slap in the face, but not that. I felt small enough to crawl into a crack between two of the soundproof tiles on the ceiling.

So much for getting a fresh start by moving to Almaden. Dad had thought that we could get away from my past by leaving the city. What a joke. A real big scream.

"Sean, wait," Nora called, but I didn't turn around. Ahead of me a young cop at a desk started to get up to stop me.

"It's all right," I heard the lieutenant say. The cop hesitated and then sat back down, watching curiously as I passed by.

Outside the station, I unlocked my bike and got it out of the rack. All I wanted to do right then was get away from there as fast as I could, so I jumped onto my bike and wheeled it out into the lot. A car screeched to a halt.

"Hey, don't you know you can get killed riding like that?"

I looked up to see a young cop sitting in a police car. He looked like he was fresh out of the police academy and eager to give someone a ticket.

Take it easy, I told myself, and above all, be polite. "I was in a hurry, officer."

"Well, you just might be in a hurry for your own funeral."

"Yes, sir. Next time I'll look both ways before riding into the lot."

He looked like he was trying to decide if I was being sarcastic or not. "I've got a good mind to give you a ticket."

But by now, another police car had swung into the lot. An older officer, with a short, gray crew cut, stuck his head out of his window. "Hey, come on, Brady. Park your car and check in."

The young cop's lips tightened as if he didn't enjoy the idea of letting any evildoer go unpunished. But he waved me on.

So I rode away. However, I couldn't help thinking what a real scream it was. I mean, in Almaden, you can get away with murder if you drive a Porsche, but don't try to ride your bike if you're a kid.

12

AFTER THE WAY NORA HAD TREATED ME, I WASN'T SURE IF I should attend the funeral Saturday or not. But it was for Marsh. I had to go no matter what Nora thought or how upset she might get.

I left Idaho and went down the stairs to the kitchen to grab a quick bite to eat. There I found Dad fussing with the automatic coffee maker. It's funny, you can give Dad a multimillion-dollar computer without a manual and he'll still figure out how to work it in a day. But give him the simplest machine and he was helpless. It was always a joke when he tried to work the automatic coffee maker. He was either doing something wrong with the filter or the coffee or the water. Now he was standing in his jogging clothes with a towel slung around his neck and a headband still soaking up his sweat—and looking awfully desperate for his fix of caffeine after all that running.

"Here, Dad," I said. "Let me do that."

"Okay, if you want to." That was one of Dad's gimmicks. He'd be there struggling away in the kitchen until you offered to help and then he'd act like you were doing it not out of pity but out of your great and undying wish to serve him. It used to drive Mom crazy, and now he was doing the same thing to me.

Dad opened the freezer door of our refrigerator, and I could hear him rummaging through the TV dinners in there (the specialty of the house). Finally, he turned to me. "Where's the frozen orange juice, sport?"

I was busy rigging up the coffee maker. "There ought to be a can in there somewhere."

"The closest thing to it is a half gallon of orange sherbert." Dad took out the carton. "And even that's almost empty." He waved it toward the list held to the refrigerator door by a little magnet. "I know you've had it hard and I don't mean to be callous, but don't you think it's time that you started getting into the swing of things again? You know you're supposed to write it down on the list when we run out of something."

That was another one of those "helpful" hints Dad had picked up from the newspaper articles. "So I forgot." I snapped on the switch to the coffee maker. "What difference does it make? I'm the only one who drinks orange juice anyway." Dad preferred to take vitamin-C pills because it was faster and more efficient.

Dad tossed the carton back into the freezer and shut the door. "For your information, we have a guest in our living room. In fact, you were just asking after him."

I didn't like the direction my imagination was taking. "Who?"

"Russ Towers." Dad waved his hand stiffly in the direction of the living room. "He's thirsty, and the only thing I've got to serve him is a can of chocolate syrup."

I almost dropped the coffeepot. "Russ? What's he doing here?" I asked dumbly.

"I met him while I was jogging in the park."

I needed time to think about what I ought to do. I forced my numb lips to move. "Okay. Okay. Why don't I bring out coffee to you?" I didn't like having to play his servant, but it was a good way to get rid of Dad.

"There's no milk." Dad made it sound grim. "What kind of impression is that going to make?"

I didn't think Dad had to worry about that too much. I think it was his son who had already made the big impression. I took out two mugs and set them down on the counter by the coffee maker. "Listen," I snapped, "you're going to have to impress him with your brains and charm, not your housekeeping skills. Not unless you want to get a job as a cook."

Dad took a deep breath and then let it out slowly as if he were counting to ten. "I keep reminding myself that you've been in a car wreck, but it's starting to wear thin as an excuse."

"Then don't do me any favors." I turned my back on Dad so I could rummage around in the cabinets for a tray.

I could hear Dad give a nervous laugh as he left the kitchen. "Kids. Nowadays they just...." And then the door swung closed and I couldn't hear Dad's words distinctly.

I leaned my head against a cabinet. Mom said that there were always plenty of choices if you just thought about a problem for a moment. I could always make the coffee and shout through the door to Dad that it was ready. Then I could take off. But how had he found me?

Was it some incredible coincidence that had brought Russ to our house? If so, then going outside was just asking for trouble because Russ would recognize me and maybe mention the library incident. And that would start a real storm.

Or was his visit more than chance? Had he come to talk to me? If that was the case—and it seemed more likely—I'd never find out if I kept running away from him. So I was probably safe enough for the moment. Though I didn't like the idea very much, I had to go outside.

When the coffee was ready, I put the mugs on the tray. I remembered the sugar and got down a box and, as a nice touch, the chocolate syrup.

Play it cool, I told myself as I backed through the swinging door. Dad and Russ must have been complaining to one another about today's kids because Russ was saying, "I never had time to play games. When my father died, all of us kids had to go to work."

"Here's the coffee," I tried to call cheerfully as I stepped into the living room. There, sitting on our sofa in a green jogging outfit, was the owner of the Porsche.

When you go to one of those horror movies, the killer or the monster always looks a little weird. I mean, maybe he's real fat or real wimpy or he's got this goofy grin. But that was the thing about Russ. If anything, he looked *too* ordinary. In fact, his face was even blander and rounder than I remembered it. Without that radar look in his eyes, he didn't look like he could kill anyone.

"You must be Sean." He smiled as if we had never seen each other. "Your father's been telling me all about you."

I picked up my cue from him. "You're Russ Towers, aren't you? Dad's told me all about you too." I forced my numb arms to set the tray down on the coffee table.

Russ slid forward so he was perched on the edge of the sofa cushion like some anxious bird. "I'm sorry to hear that you were in a car crash. I always think it's so tragic when a young person dies."

I stared at him, puzzled. He seemed sincere enough. Was he thinking of Marsh or his daughter . . . or perhaps of both? I wanted to play it real cool when I picked up the coffeepot, but my hand started to shake so bad that I had to steady it with my other hand. "That's why we have to find out more about the 'accident.'" Slowly, ever so slowly, I filled the first mug with coffee. "What'll it be? Chocolate syrup or sugar?"

"Sorry that we don't have much in the house right now." Dad was quick to apologize.

"Black will be fine," Russ said to Dad, but his eyes stayed on me all the while. "I agree with you, Sean, up to a point. But don't you think there are special cases when everyone should just forget about the past?"

My eyes couldn't help fixing on his hands as if the stains of brake fluid would still be there. But, of course, his hands and nails were meticulously clean.

Dad cleared his throat noisily to remind me that he was still waiting. "I'll take mine with sugar."

I gave my head a little shake as if I could wake up from

this nightmare. Only Russ was still there on our sofa. "Unh, sure Dad." I began to pour coffee into the second mug.

Dad tapped his fingers on the arm of his chair impatiently while he waited for his coffee. "Maybe Russ has a point. Let's say the Weisses and the truck company started arguing about who's at fault. They could all wind up in a real nasty lawsuit."

Russ took a gulp of his coffee as if it were ice cold instead of scalding hot. "Yes, reputations get blackened; lives get ruined. The only ones who really benefit from it are the lawyers."

When I had finished pouring coffee into Dad's mug, I put the coffeepot down on the tray. I wasn't sure what Russ's game was. Had he come to warn me? Why? Had Lieutenant Silva been conscientious enough to visit Russ after all? At any rate, I wasn't about to be scared off. "But people should know the truth," I said, and then looked at Dad. "I'm going to leave now if that's okay."

"That's right. Let two old bores talk shop." Dad added a spoonful of sugar to his coffee.

Russ twisted his wrist so he could glance at his watch. "Look at the time. I really should be going myself." He set his mug down on the coffee table with a thump and got to his feet. "Can I give you a lift?"

I stared at him. He couldn't really think I was crazy enough to get in a car alone with him. "No, thanks," I said, "I'll take my bike." And then, watching him intently, I added. "I'm going to the funeral for that friend who died in the car crash."

Russ winced. "Let me repeat myself. I'm truly sorry about what happened."

He sounded sincere enough. In fact, I think he could have passed a lie-detector test at that moment. "I still think I ought to take my bike."

Russ stuck his hands inside the pockets of his warm-up jacket. "You'll be safe enough," he assured me. "I'm a very safe driver."

Now I was positive that Russ hadn't met Dad by accident. No, Russ had wanted an excuse to speak with me. And I had to admit that I was curious about what he had to tell me in private. Dad would know who I was with, and I didn't think a careful man like Russ would try anything if he could be linked to it directly. The fifteen minutes it would take to the funeral chapel might be the safest fifteen minutes I would ever have.

I didn't know why he wanted to talk to me, but I'd never find out by refusing. I'd gone this far, I had to go just a little bit farther. I took a deep breath as if I were just about to dive off a cliff. "Okay," I said.

13

THE ENGINE OF THE GOLD PORSCHE ROARED INTO LIFE AND then settled into a powerful, well-tuned purring. Russ certainly took good care of his car. I might have enjoyed my first ride in a Porsche if it hadn't been for the driver.

Russ glanced at Marsh's driveway. "As God is my witness, Sean, I never meant to kill your friend. But I can do the dumbest things when I lose my temper. When I saw you two punks in a car, well...." He raised his shoulders and dipped his head in a little apologetic gesture. "I just meant to scare you boys a little and maybe teach you a lesson."

It seemed unreal to be sitting there on my sunlit street calmly holding a conversation with Marsh's murderer. I rested my right arm near the door handle so I could get away if I had to. "Like you taught the Boyer twins?"

Russ tilted his head back guiltily. "What put that into your head?"

I tried to look at him with more confidence than I felt. "I've got my sources."

Russ released the hand brake and put the car into gear. "I wondered why you were in my neighborhood. You came to snoop around with Marshal's sister...." He paused as he thought for a moment and then he snapped his fingers. "Nora, isn't it?"

I wanted to jump out of the car right then, but I told myself to stay calm. I had to find out how much he knew—for Nora's sake, if not for mine. "I wouldn't tell you whether you were right or not."

"I know I am." He pulled away from the curb with a sharp twist of the wheel. "Look, I just want to tell you that I didn't mean to hurt your friend. I figured the brake line would snap right away in the driveway like the one on the Boyers' car. How was I to know that your friend's brake line would hold that long or that he'd be driving that fast when it did go?"

Suspiciously, I studied Russ's face, but he seemed genuinely disturbed by the whole thing. I slumped down in the seat, feeling my anger begin to drain away. I didn't know who to feel sorrier for: Marsh or Russ or Russ's wife and kid. Or maybe I ought to feel sorry for this whole rotten world where things like this can happen.

I tried to remember what happened on the TV police

shows in a case like this. "Look," I said, "I'm no lawyer, but I think the worst you'd get would be manslaughter. So why don't you go to the cops and tell them what you told me."

Russ halted when the car reached El Camino. "And what would the point be? With my lawyers, I'd never even see the inside of jail." When the traffic had cleared, he turned right, taking the middle lane. "It would be a waste of the taxpayers' money."

"But people would know the truth," I reminded him.

The traffic light ahead of us turned to yellow and Russ accelerated across the intersection. "Just like you tell everyone about Mr. Rosniak, I suppose."

I reared up in the seat. "How do you know about him?"

Russ almost ran up the trunk of a slow-moving silver Toyota. Hitting his brakes, he downshifted quickly. "I have a friend who runs a collection agency. However, he's not above doing some extracurricular snooping. He's the one who traced Marsh through his license plate. And once I had the address, it wasn't any trouble to find you too. He compiled a fat file on both your families."

"So it wasn't any accident you met Dad when he was running?" I didn't know whether to be shocked or outraged.

"It was listed as a hobby on his personnel form. After that, my friend watched him and found out where he liked to run." Russ's hand coiled and uncoiled impatiently around the stick shift. "I figured that we ought to talk before this thing got out of hand."

"Scared?" I asked. I had expected him to deny it, but he gave a nervous little laugh instead.

"A little," he confessed. "But I can understand your wanting to avenge your friend."

"You're being awfully reasonable about this." Puzzled, I scratched my forehead.

"And I hope you'll be equally as reasonable." He glanced at the rearview mirror and swung out into the fast lane. "After all, what good would it do to drag my name through the mud? It won't bring your friend back to life, will it?"

"Well, no," I had to admit.

"On the other hand, I do owe you something for what happened." Russ cut back in front of the slow-moving car. "Let me help you." He swung the wheel over sharply so his car cut down a side street. "I could use a good computer man like your father. He could head up my accounting department." He inclined his head toward me. "And I could use a smart boy like you in my office. You could run errands for me." He patted the steering wheel. "You might even need to drive my Porsche as part of your duties."

Russ settled back confidently in his seat like someone who thought that everyone and everything came with a price tag and that he could afford to pay it no matter how much it cost. And then I realized why: I was probably just a thief and a liar to him.

Suddenly everything in the car felt greasy. "Maybe I'm not as smart as you think. Maybe I'm dumb and getting even dumber. But I don't think I'm going to let you buy me." I wiped my palm on the outside of the door.

"It's not as heartless as it sounds," he was quick to say. "I'm trying to learn from my mistakes, Sean. I want to be your friend." He waved his hand around as if he were offering me the entire city. "I can open a lot of doors for your father. Think of him if you won't think of yourself."

"I don't think he'd want your help either if he knew the truth." I watched the houses begin to whiz by as Russ picked up speed.

Russ straightened up in his seat as if a spring had just poked him. "I didn't have to look you up, you know." He sounded almost hurt. "But I thought it would help to tell you how sorry I am."

I watched him intently. "Sorry that Marsh is dead, or sorry that you might get caught?"

Russ was a man who was used to getting his own way. "I was just trying to do the right thing." Up ahead of us the light flashed red, but he only noticed it in the last moment and came to a screeching halt at the intersection.

We were still a half mile away from the funeral chapel, but suddenly I didn't want to risk riding with him anymore. "The right thing to do would be to confess." I put my hand on the door handle.

"It was only one moment's weakness," he said.

"And how many other weak moments are you going to have? And how many other people are you going to kill? And how many other times are you going to rationalize it all?" I swung the door open and got out.

Russ's hand clenched around the steering wheel. "I thought you were a smart boy, Sean. You disappoint me."

"I don't want anything from you—not a ride, not a job, not anything." I slammed the door shut. "You think your money can get anything for you—even justice. But it won't."

"All right then. If you won't accept my help, at least take some advice." He leaned over the seat so he could be near the passenger's window. "Forget about the car crash, Sean."

"And if I don't?" I straightened up in sullen defiance.

"An accident might happen again—either to you or to Nora."

The light had turned green by then. He sat back up and put his car into gear so he could roar across the intersection. Two strides took me to the curb. And then I started to run.

14

THE EVERGREEN FUNERAL CHAPEL WAS AN OLD-FASHIONED Victorian house—one of the few old houses in Almaden—that had been converted into a mortuary. To be honest, I was a little surprised at the turnout for Marsh's funeral. The chapel wasn't jammed to overflowing, but there were about twenty people there including Ms. Semple, Coach Lau and a few kids from school.

I was beginning to think that maybe I'd had them pegged wrong that other day when I'd thought they hadn't cared about Marsh. Even Howie was there, squeezed into a suit that he had obviously outgrown. He looked like a gray toothpaste tube about to burst. When he saw me, he twisted around to whisper to Angela, who was sitting next to him.

As I walked up the aisle, I told myself to ignore the others' stares. The important thing was to warn Nora.

There wasn't anyone in the front rows where relatives would usually sit, but Marsh had told me most of his relatives were back in New York. Instead, they were represented by wreaths of flowers so huge that the supporting stands almost seemed to bend under their weight. And in the meantime, the chapel piped in this corny song played on an organ. Between Marsh's hayfever and his taste for New Wave music, I half expected him to lift up the lid to his coffin and go storming out of the place.

I paused for a moment before the dais where the closed casket rested. It looked like a nice expensive one of polished walnut and brass. I just wish the Weisses had spent half as much on a car for Marsh as they had probably wasted on his casket.

It was hard to think that good old Marsh and his smile were underneath the lid. It seemed more likely that he was playing some joke on all of us and would appear at any moment to enjoy his funeral.

Nora and her parents were sitting in chairs to the right of the casket. Mrs. Weiss was a short, round woman weeping openly into a tattered piece of Kleenex. Her husband was older than her by about twenty years. His gray hair and mustache were carefully clipped and his suit was immaculate. He was busy blinking his eyes every now and then as if he was trying not to cry.

I held out my hand to him. "It should have been me and not him," I said to him.

"It's in God's hands," Mr. Weiss reassured me.

Mrs. Weiss looked like she was too far gone to even shake hands, so I stepped over to Nora. She had on a black pants suit with a black lace veil over her face, but even so I could see how puffy and red her eyes were.

"Nora, I'm really sorry about Marsh." I held out my hand to her.

She hesitated, then clasped my hand between both of hers for a moment and then let them drop. "I'm sure you are, Sean. So let's forget about the past." I suppose it was her way of forgiving me for what had happened yesterday.

"But that's just the point." I leaned forward, confident that she'd be apologizing to me once I told her about my ride with Russ. "Can I speak with you in private? It's real important."

She glanced at the coffin doubtfully. "I can't."

"No, dear." Mr. Weiss raised his hand and wriggled an index finger at us. "You go on."

I put a hand on Nora's elbow. "Maybe outside the chapel?"

She took a hasty step backward, away from me. "No, over there." She stepped into a little alcove to the side where a wall would hide us from those sitting in the chapel itself. It wasn't the place I would have chosen; but at least we could talk with some privacy, so I followed her over there.

"Well?" She pivoted, suspicious of some new practical joke.

I hooked my thumbs into my belt. "Russ Towers came to my house this afternoon." I added with a triumphant nod. "I think we've got him scared."

Nora screwed up her face into a mixture of pity and

disgust—as if she had just caught me wearing her underwear. "The lieutenant was right. You really do need help."

I let my hands dangle at my sides as I stared at her in surprise. I had pictured a lot of different reactions, but not this one. I guess I hadn't been willing to admit to myself that she could still doubt me. "What do you mean?"

She drew her eyebrows together angrily and frowned. "That story wasn't funny before and it's not funny now."

From the corner of my eye, I could see that the Weisses were watching us. I was sure everyone else in the chapel had turned in our direction too. "But I'm telling the truth," I whispered. "He just confessed to me that he caused the accident."

Nora's voice rose an angry octave. "Don't you know when to quit?"

Mr. Weiss started to rise from his chair, but Mrs. Weiss tugged at his sleeve and made him sit down again.

I held up my hands and motioned for Nora to stay calm. "Hey, don't make a scene," I hissed in alarm.

She flattened her hand beneath her throat and her eyes widened in disbelief. "Me? You're telling *me* not to make a scene? You're the one who's playing sick jokes."

Before this, the chapel had been stirring: people coughing, the click of purses, the rattling of odd bits of paper and so on. But now it was absolutely silent except for the piped-in music.

"I'm not joking," I protested, and my voice sounded much louder than I wanted. "That police report was ancient history. I'm not lying now."

Nora grimaced, as if I had bitten her leg, and she began to shake her head from side to side. "Get *out* of here."

I grabbed hold of Nora's arms desperately, almost as if I

were drowning right there in front of everyone. "You've got to believe me. You're in danger yourself. We both are."

But Nora was too busy wriggling and trying to push me away to listen. "Leave me alone."

Both her parents had gotten up; but it was Mr. Weiss who reached us first. "Let go of my daughter," he ordered, and gave a frantic pull at my shoulder.

Disappointed, I backed away from Nora. "You're letting Marsh's killer get away with it."

"What?" Mr. Weiss snatched his hand back.

With a worried glance at her father, Nora flew at me. "Shut up." Her hands grabbed at my shirt and she tried to swing me off the dais toward the benches. "Hasn't my family gone through enough? Why do you have to go on playing this sick game?"

I staggered a few steps. "You're the one who's sick if you won't face the truth. Russ threatened us."

Mr. Weiss looked as if I had just taken out an ax and started to chop at the coffin. His wife just stood there in a daze. But Nora flung herself at me in a cold fury. "Get out of here. Get out. Get out."

I grabbed her wrists and held her away from me as I stood sideways so that she would have a harder time kicking me. We were in full view of the others now. "You've got to believe me, Nora. You might be next on his hit list."

Coach Lau came up behind me. "Pierce. What are you doing?"

"I'm just trying to get people to see the truth," I said stubbornly. "Somebody here has to believe me. A man tampered with Marsh's car. That's why he died. And now he might go after Nora and me."

"GET OUT." Mrs. Weiss suddenly shouted. She stormed across the dais toward me. "GET OUT, YOU MONSTER."

Hastily, I let go of Nora. "Please, Mrs. Weiss." I took a step backward and found myself falling off the dais. I picked myself up quickly. "I'm only trying to...."

She stopped at the very edge of the dais, tilting her head back in almost regal wrath. "How dare you say such things." She raised her hand to slap at me but then seemed to collapse as she began to sob. "Get that boy out of here."

Coach Lau swung me around to face him. "I think you've done enough damage for one day, haven't you, Pierce?"

Helpless, I held out my hands toward him. "I'm telling the truth." But his face was cold and hard and disbelieving, so I looked beyond him toward the others. "Won't anyone listen to me?" I begged.

But there wasn't any answer. Only a room full of hostile eyes staring at me, like little invisible razor blades that were slowly cutting at me.

"Come on, Pierce." Coach Lau grabbed my arm and tried to yank me away.

I shook him off angrily. "But there's a killer on the loose and he may come after Nora and me."

Coach Lau suddenly slipped behind me and got his arms around my head in a wrestling lock. "When someone asks you to leave, Pierce, you should always take the hint." And he began to drag me down the central aisle.

"All right, all right, I'm going," I said frantically. However, the coach didn't even trust me enough to let me walk out on my own.

"We're going to talk about this at school," he growled

ominously. I just bet. And with him would be the vice-principal and Ms. Semple and probably a whole bunch of others. Grown-ups like going after a kid—especially when they're in a pack. "You've pulled just one too many jokes."

"But I'm telling the truth," I repeated, my voice rising on a whining note that even I didn't like.

"We don't like troublemakers here." He thrust me into the hallway.

"That's right. You don't want anyone to rock the boat. You want to sail on in a nice, snug little world where you ignore the truth if it's unpleasant."

Coach Lau started toward me again with righteous menace, like a wildcat protecting its cubs. "I'm going to talk to your father."

"Sure. You might as well all gang up on me." But I backed down the hallway toward the doors.

I had thought that the *Rocky Horror Picture Show* was pretty weird. It's strange to find out that the horror show can be for real.

15

DAD WASN'T AT HOME WHEN I GOT BACK. THERE WAS A NOTE on the refrigerator saying that he had gone to do some shopping. I tore up the note before I threw it into the sink. Then I walked over to the telephone on the kitchen wall and began to dial Seattle. I just hoped Neil wasn't there. I wanted someone "real" to talk to.

"Hello?" said a young girl.

"Hey, Caitlin." I leaned my elbow on the kitchen counter. "This is Sean. Remember me?"

"Sean?" Her voice grew brighter, as if she was actually

happy to hear me, and that made a nice contrast to the good people of Almaden. "Mom got the tickets."

"Tickets?"

"To the concert. Remember? You asked Mom to get them for when you were visiting us?"

"Oh, yeah, sure." I was supposed to fly up for the month of July with Mom and Caitlin. But somehow rock concerts and vacations seemed very remote now, like strange rituals the natives practiced in New Guinea.

"Is something wrong?" Caitlin's voice changed. She was pretty sharp for an eleven-year-old. "You sound like you're having hard times."

"Unh, well, yeah," I said, embarrassed.

"That's what happens when I'm not there to check up on you." Caitlin sounded very sure of herself.

"I don't think even you could have helped this time." I shifted my weight to my other foot. "Is Mom around?"

"She's taking a nap before she goes to the center. But I'll wake her." She dropped the receiver so that it banged against the wall. I held my own receiver away from my ear.

I had a few anxious minutes waiting by the phone, drumming my fingers on the counter. The sound of soft, anxious voices came from a distance. And then I could hear the shuffling of Mom's furry slippers. It was an old, familiar sound and it made me wish I was a lot younger and had never gotten into trouble and was up in Seattle with her, instead of stuck down here with Dad.

She still sounded pretty drowsy when she spoke into the phone. "Yes? What's the matter, Sean?"

I ran a frustrated hand through my hair. "People, Mom. Just people. They can be so dense sometimes."

"They can be, can't they?" Mom agreed.

I slapped my hand against my side. "I mean, you try and tell them the truth and they think you're crazy."

It was the wrong word to use. Mom instantly became alert. "Why? What's going on?"

I shook my head. "Mom, don't start getting professional on me."

"I'm sorry, dear. I guess it's a conditioned reflex." Was it my imagination, or was Mom just a little too quick to apologize?

It's a funny thing about telephones. You can hear the other person at the end of the line but you can't touch them. They're just bodiless voices—like ghosts. Maybe if I could have seen Mom's face, I would have felt like I was talking to my mother instead of to a professional counselor. "Yeah, I guess it happens. Have things been busy at the center."

"It seems to come in cycles sometimes," Mom said cautiously.

"But what causes a lot of people to call up? A lost football game? A stock-market crash? A full moon? What?" I was rambling, but I couldn't help it.

"It's a number of factors." Mom was speaking slowly, as if she were weighing and calculating my every word. "But what about you, dear?"

I pulled at the phone cord. "It's a mess, Mom. Even worse than last time."

"Oh?" was all that Mom said.

I blurted out desperately. "I don't know which way to turn."

"Whatever is wrong, you'll feel much better talking about it, dear."

I scratched the back of my neck nervously. "Well, is it

crazy to think that a car crash may not have been an accident?"

"Of course not," Mom reassured me. "But you would need some pretty solid evidence or people probably wouldn't believe you."

I rubbed my chin. "Evidence?"

"Yes, dear. When a charge is that serious, you need real proof." Mom's tone was warm and friendly: just the right thing to soothe everyone but a child of hers. I knew the tone was fake.

I gave a snort. "I guess *my* word wouldn't be good enough."

"Whom do you suspect, dear?" Mom coaxed.

"Russ Towers." And I added quickly in my defense. "You know how tough he can be, Mom."

Mom only hesitated a second or so. "Yes, I do, dear." To give her credit, she sounded worried. "He is not the kind of man whom I would care to cross."

I was beginning to think that Mom believed me after all. "Well, I think he's got this bug against kids with cars now—which I can kind of understand."

"But . . . why is he mad at you?" Mom wondered.

So I told Mom about the tire prank and everything else that had happened since then, including the chat with Russ. "But when I tried to tell Nora at the funeral, she thought I was joking," I finished up. "I mean, like I was really some sick, weird person."

"Have you spoken to the police?"

"Yes." I leaned my head to the side, holding the phone receiver between my ear and my shoulder. "But they wouldn't believe me." I swallowed and muttered. "You know why."

"Yes," Mom sighed. I could hear Caitlin's anxious voice in the background. "Excuse me for a moment, dear," she said to me. I could hear their muffled voices but not their words—Mom must have put her hand over the receiver so I couldn't eavesdrop on their conversation. Then she came back on. "Dear," she said, forcing herself to be cheerful, "why don't you fly up here and let's talk about it."

"Is that Caitlin's idea or yours?"

"The invitation is from the both of us." Mom sounded hurt that I could be suspicious of her. "Please come. We'd love to see you."

It would have been so easy to say yes. I wanted to get away from Almaden almost more than anything else. Almost. There was still one thing that was more important.

"Do you think I'm telling the truth?" I had to ask.

"I don't think you're lying," Mom answered diplomatically.

"At least not consciously, is that it?" I felt empty inside, so empty that my shoulders sagged. Mom didn't have any more faith in me than the others did. She was trying to protect me not from Russ but from myself. The words came out of me in a bitter flood. "Yeah, I see: Slip up once and the world thinks you're a liar every time. But as long as you have money, you can get away with murder."

"Sean," Mother said quietly, "you only hurt yourself when you think like that."

I shifted the phone receiver to my other ear. "Did you tell Caitlin what I told you?"

"A little."

"Did she think I was crazy too?" It was important that Caitlin believe me.

"Wait a moment, dear." There was a pause while I heard more muffled conversation, and this time it definitely had an anxious edge to it. Then Caitlin was fumbling at the receiver.

"You come up on the first plane, you hear me?" She sounded worried.

"Why?" I tried to joke. "So you can keep an eye on your moron of a brother?"

"No," Caitlin said indignantly. "We miss you."

I lowered the receiver and stared at the mouthpiece. I guess she figured I was having some kind of nervous breakdown. Great. Just what I needed—to be treated like Mad Dog Sean.

"Sean? Sean?" Caitlin called insistently.

I brought the receiver back up. "No, it's okay. You two don't have to keep an eye on me. I'll just tough it out down here."

"Honestly," Caitlin said in exasperation, "you can be so pigheaded sometimes."

"We've got the same genes," I reminded her. "Suddenly I heard the familiar rattle of Dad's keys in the locks to the front door. "Oh-oh. Dad's here," I said. "I think I'd better hang up."

"Wait, Sean," Caitlin said urgently. "I think Mom and I want to talk to Dad."

"Unh ... yeah, sure," I mumbled. I waited miserably until the front door opened. "Dad," I called, "Caitlin would like to talk to you."

Dad entered the kitchen eagerly and set his bag of groceries down on the floor. "Really?" He held out his hand for the phone receiver. But I couldn't help turning Russ's warning over and over in my head. What had he meant about accidents happening again? Did he intend to strike at me by hurting Dad? Would he tamper with the brakes like he had tampered with Marsh's?

I slipped into the garage where the bright yellow mover's cartons covered the concrete floor. Dad could park his car inside if we just piled them to one side, so I began to stack the boxes on top of one another.

When Dad came into the garage fifteen minutes later, he had this look on his face as if he had just found out I had sold all of his secret notes to the Russians. "What's the idea of calling your mom with that wild story? You've gotten her so worried that she was going to take a leave of absence and fly down here with Caitlin."

I hefted one carton that felt like it had forty pounds of rocks in it. The words just slipped out before I could think of what I was saying. "Well, at least we'd be together again."

Dad folded his arms over the jacket of his jogging suit. "But Russ Towers?" The phone rang. "We're not finished yet," he promised, and then, being the closest, he went to answer it.

Though Dad's voice was muffled by the door, I could just hear him say hello to Coach Lau. When he came out a moment later, he looked ready to lynch me.

"Great." I turned to the next carton. "I can see I won't have to wait till the Fourth of July for fireworks."

Dad stepped around in front of me. "You don't know what trouble is. You're grounded as of"—he glanced at his wristwatch—"six forty-eight."

I was getting tired of being shoved around. "What are you going to do, Dad? Chain me to my bed?"

Dad leaned against the wall of cartons I was building. "What's gotten into you, sport?"

I squatted down by the last carton. "I'm not a 'sport.' Why can't you use my name like I was a human being?"

Dad stiffened. "It's just an affectionate name. I didn't think...."

"My name's Sean," I said firmly. "You gave me that name. Please use it."

Frowning, Dad came over and set one foot on top of the carton so I couldn't lift it. "Okay. Your mother was always saying that I never listened to what people were saying." He tucked his hands into the pockets of his jacket. "So why don't you tell me your story?"

Not daring to hope for much, I told Dad everything from the prank with the tires up to the moment I left Marsh's funeral. When I was finished, I looked at Dad defensively. "No one seems to believe what I have to say. Just because he's rich and just because I've gotten into trouble before this."

Dad jerked his head at me. "There's just one thing wrong with your story. Why would an important man like Russ go around terrorizing kids?"

"You said yourself that no one messes with him," I reminded Dad. "Maybe not even pranksters."

Dad lowered his foot to the ground and stared at the tip of his running shoe as if he could find all the answers to our problems right there. Finally, he shook his head as if he were just totally lost. "I think you'd better see Dr. Arneson." He was a psychiatrist who lived down the block and a tennis buddy of Dad's.

I glared at him. "I don't need a shrink."

Dad raised his hands apologetically. "It was your mother's idea."

I lifted the last carton and slid it onto the others. "I just need someone to trust me. The truth is not something that you reach by majority vote, you know."

Dad ran his hands over his face. "Sometimes I think I need an interpreter when I talk to you." When he finally dropped his hands, he stared as if he had just noticed what was going on. "What are you doing anyway?"

I gestured toward the garage door. "I thought you might want to park your car inside from now on. Your friend, Russ, told me that accidents could happen again."

"I don't know if I should encourage you any more." He looked as if he were ready to cart me over to Dr. Arneson's that very moment.

"All right. *Don't* drive it in." I started for the garage door in a cold fury. "I'll push it in for you if I have to."

Impressed, Dad joined me by the door. "You're really upset by the idea of leaving the car outside, aren't you?"

I unbolted the door. "I'm just trying to protect you, whether you like it or not."

"I guess you are in your way, Sp . . . I mean, Sean." Dad seemed touched by my concern for his safety.

"As crazy as it may seem to you, I really do care." I set my shoulder against the door.

"Well, I suppose my car would start easier if it wasn't left outside." Impulsively, he added his shoulder to the door and together we shoved it up.

When we had parked the car on the inside, I rebolted the door, feeling a bit more secure.

Dad leaned out of his window. "What am I going to do with you?"

"I don't know," I said truthfully.

16

DAD DIDN'T LOSE ANY TIME CALLING DR. ARNESON, WHO SAID he would be happy to see me Monday afternoon. I left them while they were still chatting on the phone. I had a lot of thinking I wanted to do.

I hadn't really expected too much from Dad, who was out of his depth when things couldn't be put into a flow chart. I'd felt bad when the kids had turned against me, and it had really hurt when Nora joined them. But I'd felt even worse when Mom and Caitlin had sided with them too.

I sulked for a long while up in Idaho, feeling just as alone as if I were the last boy on earth. What made the isolation seem even worse was the fact that it wasn't anything as complicated as a plague or a magical curse that had left me so isolated. It was something as simple and pure and deadly as the truth.

When I finally got right down to it, I realized that life hadn't changed all that much since people lived in caves. Go against the tribe and you get tossed out of the cave away from the light and the warmth and the laughter. And there you were, alone with the stars and the moon and a darkness so cold that it could chill you down to your very bones.

Half of me wanted to crawl back to them and apologize, say they were right and please wouldn't they let me back in? I suppose in the old days they would have sent out a witch doctor to make me eat dirt and then splash some purifying water over me. But nowadays, we did it more neatly by going to a shrink. And after a few sessions, all I had to do was play the clown like all the rest of them and I'd be accepted back into the circus.

I remembered what Marsh had told me: When we let other people pull our strings, we die inside—bit by bit, day by day until nothing's left but a body as soulless as a bunch of wooden blocks tied together with strings. No, I couldn't go crawling back to the others.

And suddenly I knew what I had to do. If I could just get my hands on that file on Marsh and me that Russ had talked about, I'd be able to prove that there was a connection between Russ and myself. Maybe I could even get the name of Russ's friend at the collection agency. At the very least, there ought to be handwritten notes.

I imagined everyone's face—including Lieutenant

Silva's—when I waved a memo with my name and Marsh's written on the paper in Russ's handwriting. I was sure the police would come up with other things on Russ once they started digging.

When I heard the car motor outside, I glanced at the clock. I'd been meditating in Idaho for almost three hours. The car seemed awfully close, so I went to the window.

It was the Weisses, back from the funeral. Mr. Weiss went on ahead to open the door while Mrs. Weiss followed, leaning on Nora.

I tried to see what happened, but I couldn't stick my head out the window because it was louvered like all the other windows in our house. Instead of one big pane of glass, there were all these long, narrow rectangular slats of glass overlapping one another; so all I could do was press my face against the glass and watch until I thought I saw the lights go on in Nora's room upstairs.

And I knew I couldn't hide up in Idaho anymore. I had to warn Nora about any possible fallout.

I went to the bedroom door and glanced downstairs. The TV wasn't on, so I figured Dad was probably in his study working on some project and trying to forget his crazy son.

I tiptoed down the carpeted steps and out the front door. Now that the sun had set, it was cold outside, and I shivered, hugging myself as if I could keep my own warmth inside that way.

I walked over to our driveway and looked at the Weisses' house. The light was on in Nora's room. I went over to the hyacinths and got a pebble from the dirt to throw against the window. The Weisses had louvered windows too, and the pebble rattled against one of the panes.

When Nora didn't appear right away, I went and got a handful of pebbles, intending to use them all until I got to see her again.

She finally came to her window after I'd thrown up the sixth pebble. She frowned when she saw it was me.

She pulled at the lever which made the louvered panes tilt outwards at a ninety-degree angle. When she spoke, she made an elaborate show of enunciating each syllable slowly and carefully. "Go away."

I looked up at her. "We've got to talk. It's important."

She studied me for a moment and then lifted her head slightly. "You had your say."

"Please come down." I held out my hands helplessly from my sides. "I'll go crazy if I don't speak to you."

She had this look on her face like she didn't think I had very far to go; but she was a good enough person to want to help. "Wait a moment," she finally said, and left her window. Several anxious minutes later, the front door opened and Nora stepped outside. "My parents are in their bedroom, but either one of them could come downstairs at any time. So make it quick."

I swallowed. "First of all, I'm sorry about the funeral."

She eyed me warily, as if she was ready to bolt back into her house at the first sign of trouble. "That's good for a start."

I dipped my head. "And I'm going to see Dr. Arneson. He's a shrink."

"Oh, Sean, that's the best news ever." On some sudden impulse, Nora threw her arms around me and gave me a warm hug. "The first step in dealing with a problem is recognizing that you have one."

I didn't return her hug, though. "I'm going because my

dad wants me to. The problem isn't in my head. It's in everyone else's."

Nora stepped back, but she kept her hands on my arms. "Don't worry. We'll all be there to help you. There are a lot of people who care about you, Sean."

"Sure." I couldn't help the bitterness that crept into my voice. "Just like the audience at a freak show gives money to stop birth defects."

Her fingers tightened around my arms. "You scare me when you talk like that."

But I looked over her shoulder toward the Weisses' station wagon. "You don't know what it really means to be frightened," I said to her. "Not until you have everyone turn against you."

Nora wrinkled her forehead in puzzlement. "I don't understand why you wanted to talk to me."

"I just wanted to tell you to be real careful." I watched her intently. "And if something happens to me, then go to the cops."

Nora snatched her hands back, curling her fingers as if she had just been burnt. "What are you going to do?"

"Nora," I said quietly, "do you remember what you told me at the library? You said someone has to take a stand, even if it starts with only one person."

Nora looked stunned. "That was about big issues like nuclear disarmament."

"Do you think Washington, D.C., is the only place where people lie?" I demanded. "Nora, Russ is the liar, not me. And I'm going to get the proof I need."

"Sean, don't do anything wild." She started to reach her hand out toward me, but I ducked away.

"It's a little late for that," I laughed harshly.

Nora looked at me in a worried, hurt way. "It's never too late. You make us sound like a pack of wolves."

"More like a bunch of puppeteers after the runaway puppet."

"What?" She pulled her head back.

"It's just something that your brother told me," I explained. "Only I didn't believe him then." I started to back away from her. "Now remember." I shook my index finger at her. "Be ultracautious this week. It's either Russ or us."

She started to follow me. "Sean, I. . . ."

I waved her back into her house. "Just humor me, okay? Play it real safe." And I turned around.

I knew I could probably find the evidence in Russ's home. The only problem was that I'd promised Dad I wouldn't break into any more houses. Still, if Dad found out, he probably wouldn't think any worse of me. I was probably as low as I could get in his opinion, right down there with the chain-saw murderers and cannibals. And at least I would be trying to do something about Marsh's death.

As I headed back toward my house, my mind began running over the things that I'd need. And inside I felt a strange kind of peace: as if from now on I was going to slide through the world knife-smooth, just like Marsh had wanted me to.

17

I PLAYED IT REAL COOL MONDAY. WHEN I WENT TO SCHOOL, I concentrated on being just like a shadow. The other kids treated me as if I had the Black Death, but I pretended I didn't care. And when I had my promised session with Ms. Semple, Coach Lau and the others, I acted like the good, meek little boy who has learned his lesson. The only rough spot came when I tried to switch my appointment with Dr. Arneson to another day. The receptionist really dug around for my reasons, but in the end she did what I asked.

When school was finally over, I headed straight for Russ's neighborhood. I saw a couple of kids on the streets, but they were moving slowly toward their homes. I stopped about a block away from Russ's and locked my bike. Then, tucking a clipboard under my arm, I started for his house. Sometimes kids went around trying to sign people up for lawn-care outfits so I figured I could use that line if anyone asked me what I was doing there.

When I rounded the corner, I could see that the curtains were drawn on Russ's windows and his car wasn't in the driveway. My heard began to pound louder and faster than a cheap, rebuilt engine, and my legs suddenly felt like they had twenty pounds of ankle weights strapped to them.

I concentrated on taking several long, deep breaths, telling myself that this was going just like I had rehearsed it in my mind all last Saturday night. Step by step, I forced my legs up the driveway, though it almost felt as if I were trying to move through glue.

I rang the doorbell good and hard and long; and when no one came to the door, I tried ringing even harder and longer. When there still wasn't any answer, I started to walk across the lawn like I was taking a shortcut to the next house.

I paused, though, by the gate that led into Russ's backyard. Kneeling, I pretended to tie my shoe, but it was really to give me a chance to scan the neighborhood. There wasn't a soul in sight. Pitching the clipboard over the gate, I caught hold of the redwood boards. They were thin, almost wobbling under my hands; but they held long enough for me to pull myself up and over.

I landed hard on the flagstones, feeling it mainly in my numbed feet. I waited, holding my breath, but no one demanded to know what I was doing there. I followed the flagstones past the three dented garbage cans to the side of the path and then the chimney at the side of the house.

The lawn in the back was more weeds than grass, and the lawn and bushes were mostly brown, killed by too much sun and not enough water. At one end of the lawn, a lone tree thrust bare, leafless branches straight up at the sky. Underneath the tree was one of those jungle-gym sets, the kind with the little swing and ladder and all. It was the last thing I expected to see in Russ's backyard.

I was drawn to the gym set. The seat of the swing hung pretty low, as if it was meant for a kid about nine or ten. And here was the weird thing: it had just been freshly painted, and the chains that held the swing and other things were brand new. There wasn't a speck of rust on them. I nudged the seat with my foot and it swung back and forth slowly. Was he trying to keep it in good shape for her ghost?

I got this real strange feeling, like the hairs at the back of my neck had come alive. Somewhere someone was watching a quiz show on TV. I could hear the game-show host rattling off a list of prizes and I was almost grateful for that familiar sound.

Part of me wanted to leave right then. What weird things would I see inside his house? What right did I have to invade his privacy like this? But then I remembered Marsh. What right did Russ have to kill him? I had to go through it—for Marsh's sake if not for mine. Reaching my hand underneath my jacket, I got the heavy screwdriver from the waistband of my jeans.

It was easy to take off the screws to the window screen. The window itself was one of those sliding affairs—the kind I used to love when I was ripping off houses. I dug around with the screwdriver, working it between the window and the frame. It took me a little longer because I was out of practice, but I felt the screwdriver catch. With a quick jerk of my wrists, I jimmied the window open. There was a snap as the cheap lock broke.

I put the screwdriver away and took my gloves from my back pocket. Well, actually, they were a pair of mittens this aunt in Minnesota had sent me. For some reason she'd gotten it into her head that I was only twelve so she'd knitted a pair of mittens with snowflakes and reindeer on them. I pulled them on now, feeling a little foolish as the wool stretched. The reindeer twitched as I wriggled my hand.

I'd had to use the mittens because Dad would have become suspicious if he'd noticed I'd taken his work gloves; but he hadn't missed the screwdriver because he had so many of them. And anyway, the main thing was not to leave prints. I boosted myself through the open window and found myself looking into a bathroom. There was a toilet right underneath me, and across from it was a pink bathtub that matched the pink shower curtains and rug.

Gripping the frame, I pulled myself far enough through the window to get first one leg and then the other onto the toilet seat. There were pink towels hanging on the racks and a pink bar of scented soap in the dish by the faucet. Somehow I didn't think it was Russ's idea of decor. Maybe it was his dead wife's.

The air seemed still and lifeless in there, as still and lifeless as a museum I'd visited once. They had a whole reconstruction of what it was like to enter a pyramid where they buried Pharaohs. Russ's house had that same tomb-like feeling.

I opened the door and listened carefully, but there

wasn't a sound. I could feel a sudden rush of adrenaline that made my heart beat faster, and it was harder to take regular breaths. It was bad to feel that excitement at breaking into a house—it made me feel, well, if not good, then really alive.

I followed the hallway a short distance into the living room. It must have been a pretty comfortable place once. The sofas were those heavy, thickly padded kind, and there were a lot of pictures and decorations on the wall—including a couple of kid's drawings in glass frames. By the sofa, though, was a pair of little sneakers. They were about half the size of my feet so I was sure they belonged to Russ's daughter. The white shoelaces of both sneakers were still tied in knots and one of them lay on its side as if they had just been kicked off. I had this hunch that the sneakers had lain that way for a long time beside a case full of fashion dolls.

There was a bunch of doll furniture within walls constructed from wooden blocks and there were dishes and cups on the table as if the dolls had been waiting all these years for their dinner.

I guess people hadn't realized just how upset Russ was after his family died. But it wasn't really all that crazy when I started to think about it. I suppose it was a way of keeping their memories fresh and alive for himself.

I mean, the emperor of India built the Taj Mahal. This was a smaller, quieter, more private kind of monument. It's funny, but a little thought keep nagging at me. Would Dad have mourned for me like this if I'd died in that car crash? I shook off the question. Of course, he wouldn't have. There are few people who would. I turned away, trying to keep my mind on the business at hand.

Against one wall was a set of expensive wooden

shelves with a lot of fancy audio equipment and speakers. By the shelves was a padded leather chair with a footrest and next to it was a pile of newspapers.

On a hunch, I went over to them and I started to go through them. They weren't in any special order so it took me a moment before I found the right one. Marsh's accident had been too late to make the Sunday paper, but there had been a little five-line paragraph at the very back of the Monday edition. I turned the pages until I found the page where the article should have been—only I was staring through a hole.

I'd really only hoped to get the file that Russ had on Marsh and me, but maybe he was methodical enough to have kept a file on the accident. Maybe there'd even be notes on his plans for sabotaging Marsh's car. I had to find Russ's study.

I went back to the hallway and tried a door on my right, but it was only a closet with a vacuum cleaner and a lot of liquor bottles. The next one opened into a bedroom with a pair of men's pajamas laid over the carefully made bed. Apparently Russ was one of those people who liked everything neat and in its place.

That left the two doors on the other side of the hallway. When I opened the first one, I felt a surge of triumph. I'd found his study. It was going to take quite a while to search it because there were so many filing cabinets. I'd have to work quickly; but for the first time in days, I began to think that I just might be able to squirm out of this mess I'd gotten into.

Eagerly, I stepped into the room, and bright lights winked on, blinding me for a moment. I gave a shout and held my arms up over my eyes while a loud alarm began whooping. I felt like I was on the bridge of a Navy ship being strafed by Japanese Zeros.

"What is this?" I muttered, and tried to shield my eyes with my hands. I managed to make out the kind of lights that the drama teacher used when he was videotaping. I looked down dumbly and saw that I was standing right in the middle of an electric-eye beam.

I looked wildly around the room and saw the video camera mounted above the desk near the ceiling. The lens was pointed straight at my stupid, gaping face. I swore at myself for being such a spacehead. The one room that a president of an electronics firm would want to guard would be his study. After all, there were all sorts of news stories about industrial spies in this area.

I looked around for the videotape recorder in the wild hope that I could get to it and take the incriminating tape. But a cable led from the camera into a wall. The recorder could have been hidden in the attic or in the walls someplace. I wouldn't have put anything past Russ.

At any rate, I didn't have time to find the tape. The burglar alarm was whooping too loud. One of the neighbors was bound to call the cops, if only to complain about the noise. I went back out through the bathroom, got my clipboard and stripped off the mittens.

Then I went back over the fence. No one called out. The houses on Russ's street were still locked up tight.

I wanted to run, but I forced myself to walk as if I had every right to be there. There was still no one watching as I crossed the lawn to the sidewalk. Taking my time, I strolled along the sidewalk to my bike.

Then I slowly cycled along the street, pausing curiously like any other kid would have, when I passed Russ's house. The alarm was still sounding, and two people stood now on the opposite side of the street. One was a man in bright turquoise Bermuda shorts and the other was a woman in a red and orange muumuu with a pattern that looked like she had sat on some artist's palette. They were talking and gesturing at the house.

With one last look at Russ's place, I hurried home.

18

I WAITED FOR ABOUT AN HOUR FOR THE COPS TO COME. WHEN they didn't, I tried to figure it out. By now someone must have told Russ about the break-in. He would have seen the videotape, complete with instant replays and stop action. So why hadn't the police come with dogs and chains to take me away?

And then I realized what an idiot I'd been. If Russ told the police about my break-in, they would have to start an investigation. After all, if I was so worked up that I would risk jail, there might be something behind my story.

In fact, I should have stayed at Russ's house searching for the file until the cops came. If I had the folder in my hands, they would have to take it along with me. And then the police would have to start checking out my story and people would start to realize that Russ's solid-gold reputation was really brass. Now it was too late. Russ had more than enough time to destroy the file and cover his tracks.

I jumped when I heard the phone ring. I thought it might be Russ or the cops, but it was Mom.

"Hi, I just thought I'd see how you two were doing." There was a professional warmth to her voice.

I really wanted to tell her about what I had found at Russ's. But I could guess what her reaction would be: her poor, crazy son had really taken a dive off the deep end this time. I'd have to wait till the truth came out. "Oh, we're doing okay. In fact, great."

"And how did it go with Dr. Arneson?" Mom tried to ask casually.

Mom was fishing for something, but I didn't know for what. "Fine," I said nervously.

Mom picked up on that right away. "If you're not comfortable with him, we can find someone else."

"No, I think I'll give him a chance." I shifted the receiver over to my other ear as if that could somehow magically throw Mom off the track.

The words came rushing out of Mom as if she couldn't control her worries. "But he is a friend of your father's and that may not be a good thing."

It's funny. All this time and all this distance hadn't ended the war between Dad and Mom. "No, Mom," I said firmly. "He's okay." Or I guess he would be.

"But...." Mom began to protest.

"Mom," I said in frustration, "just give it up, will you?"

"Don't use that tone of voice with me, young man," Mom snapped. "I'm trying to protect you."

"Well, you can't do it long-distance," I said angrily. "It was bad enough when we were still under the same roof and you and Dad used to argue about what was best for us."

"We were thinking of you." Mom sounded hurt.

"Oh, sure," I said sarcastically. "Just like two generals worry about the field where they're going to fight."

"I wish you wouldn't exaggerate, dear." But Mom didn't seem as confident as before.

I suppose I should have shut up but I couldn't help it. I had kept all the bitterness inside me too long. I gripped the receiver a little tighter. "Just tell me one thing, will you?"

"Whatever you want, dear."

"Why did you leave me behind with Dad?"

Mom was a little defensive. "Well, I wanted you to come to Seattle with me, but your father was so firm about your staying with him." Her voice took on a brittle edge. "You'll have to ask him for his reasons."

"If I can," I said.

"Exactly," Mom said. "The intricacies of human feelings are as incomprehensible to your father as a flow chart is to me."

But I'd had enough warfare for one day. "I guess so," I said lamely. "Well, I've got to go. Thanks for calling."

"All right, dear," Mom said. "And feel free to call me anytime you like. Collect if you have to."

"Yes, bye." And I hung up the phone quickly.

I told myself that I couldn't let family matters distract me. I had Russ on the defensive; he was more afraid of the police than I was. I had to figure out another way of getting solid evidence on him.

I still hadn't come up with a new plan by the time Dad pulled into the driveway and turned off the car engine. And then, as if he thought he ought to humor me, he opened up the garage door and got back into his car. The engine started again and he drove the car inside.

When he stepped into the house, he made a point of saying my name. "S-ea-n."

"I'm in the living room, Dad." I had purposely sat in the recliner so he couldn't sit next to me. "I didn't go to Dr. Arneson's."

"I know." I thought he'd be mad enough to chew nails, but he only looked at me kind of worried. "They called me at work when you changed your appointment." He slung his attaché case onto the sofa and plopped down beside it. "Do you mind telling me why?"

I studied Dad warily. He would have been ranting about Russ's house if he had known about it. Apparently, Russ wanted to keep things ultrasecret. I was beginning to feel like the cards were finally starting to fall my way now. But in the meantime I had to deal with Dad.

"You made the appointment, Dad, not me." I shook my head for emphasis. "I don't need to see a shrink."

"But you do." Dad clapped his hands on his knees. "Half of being an adult is knowing when you need help."

It was a nasty thing to say, but I couldn't help it. The conversation with Mom had set me to thinking. "Like with you and Mom?"

Dad rocked back as if I had just kicked him in the stomach. "Counseling wouldn't have helped us. People sometimes . . . grow away from one another."

"But the way you used to argue, Caitlin and I used to

think it was our fault." Somehow I found myself blurting out the words. "Mom used to say we were watching too much TV and you used to say it was harmless. Or you used to say I ought to try Pop Warner football and she used to say I ought to read more. It seemed like what one of you wanted for us kids, the other didn't."

"I guess both you and Caitlin got caught in the middle." Dad slumped back against the sofa, suddenly looking very tired. "I'm sorry Sean."

I forced the recliner to tilt backward. An apology was the last thing I'd ever expected to hear from Dad—because he was always trying to act like he was the perfectly programmed human being. Encouraged, I finally blurted out, "Why did you want me to stay with you? Was it so Mom couldn't have me?"

Dad sat upright. "Whatever made you think that?" He held up a hand suddenly. "No, I don't think I want to hear. It might be too long a list." He dropped his hand down on top of his attaché case and shook his head. "It's just that I've made so many mistakes, Sean. There was that time I played it safe instead of going with Russ. And then there was the trouble with my own business. And then your Mom." He raised his hands, palms upwards. "But I had hopes that if I did one thing right in my life it would be raising you."

I found myself pitying Dad. "I'm sorry I've been such a big disappointment."

He leaned forward urgently. "It's not your fault at all." He pressed a hand against his chest. "It's mine, Sean. I mean, if the bond between us had been stronger, maybe we would have been doing more and you wouldn't have gotten into trouble."

To my surprise, I found myself trying to comfort him.

"Dad, you can't take the blame for what I did. You didn't shove me through the window into someone else's house."

"That was a cry for help." Dad repeated my regular shrink's favorite phrase. "And I should have created a climate where you didn't need to steal." Dad gave a little shrug. "Well, at least you have to give me points for being consistent: I seem to fail at everything I do."

Dad looked so miserable that I felt like I had to say something. "But I'm the real failure, Dad."

Dad's head shot up and he looked at me sternly. "I don't want to hear that kind of talk from you. You're young. You have your whole life ahead of you."

"Well, so do you," I tossed back at him.

"I'm fifty years old," he reminded me. "And computing is really a young man's game. It's too late now for me to become something."

"But there are plenty of opportunities..." I began.

"For you, maybe, but not for me." Dad bit the words out. "I was lucky to get the job I have, even if I'm only a glorified 'gofer.'"

I swallowed. "It must be hard for you."

Dad's hand clenched into a fist. "I don't ever want you to feel the way I do."

It was strange to realize that Dad had his own phantoms haunting him. Whether it was true or not, Dad felt like a has-been. If there was any way that I could have turned back the clock for him and made him younger, I would have. As it was, I could only try to make things a little easier for him. "Look, if it'll make you feel any better, I'll keep the next appointment with Dr. Arneson."

Dad scratched his throat for a moment. "Well, they say

it takes two to tango." He smiled suddenly. "Why don't I go with you?"

"Together?" I asked, shocked.

"Or separately." Dad spread out his hands. "Whatever he suggests."

I blinked my eyes. "Why?"

Dad looked straight at me. "Because I'd like you to stay, Sean. I don't want you to feel like you have to leave." He ground his fist into his knee. "All right, so maybe things didn't work out with your mother. I'd at least like to arrange something between us."

"Yeah, okay, Dad." I was beginning to feel a faint glimmer of hope when the phone rang.

Dad smiled at me weakly. "The world just doesn't seem to want to leave us alone, does it?" He got up as the phone rang a second time.

I could feel how clammy my hands were getting as the phone rang a third and then a fourth time. Dad had left the kitchen door open in his rush to get the phone, so I could hear him talk.

"Oh, yes, Albert. How are you?" Dad said. I sighed with relief; it wasn't Russ after all. Albert was the Kid, Dad's boss. "This is rather short notice, sir.... Well, thank you, sir. It's nice to hear you say I'm the best man for the job, but I do have a family...." Dad sounded hesitant. "Well, yes, Albert. I know they have a big contract with us." Dad's voice grew tight and hard as he answered "Yes" several more times. I guess the Kid was laying down the law to him. He hung up the receiver with a sigh and came back in.

"Sean, I ..." he began.

"The Kid's on your case again, isn't he, Dad?" I wanted

to help him get off the hook as easily as possible.

Dad let out an exasperated sigh. "There's a problem with a client in LA, and I have to go down there to troubleshoot."

"Well," I said, trying to find something good about it. "Didn't he say you were the best man for the job?"

"Oh, he was just trying to snow me," Dad shrugged. "He knows I'm the employee who can least afford to complain." Still, he seemed to be pleased.

"So when do you go?" I got up from the chair.

"Tonight. There's a nine o'clock flight." He stood there uncertainly for a moment. "But I don't know if I ought to leave you alone at a time like this."

Poor Dad. I knew that the Kid hadn't given him much choice about going. The only way Dad could stay here was if he actually quit. "Hey, don't worry about me, Dad. I'm old enough to take care of myself." I gave him an encouraging grin. "You may even find the bottle bush trimmed when you come home."

Dad broke into a broad smile. "Let's both work on that bush. Why should you have all the fun?"

"You got yourself a deal," I said.

Okay, so it wasn't a total victory, but at least it was a start. He was trying to reach out to me and I was trying to reach out to him. Maybe we'd make more solid contact eventually—if I lived that long.

19

I DON'T KNOW WHAT WOKE ME UP IN THE MIDDLE OF THE NIGHT but I came awake almost instantly alert.

I glanced over at the digital clock on the nightstand. The red numbers seemed to burn in the darkness; it was all of three A.M.

I got up and opened the door to Idaho and saw a flash of light below. Dad's flight must have been cancelled or maybe he forgot something that he needed. "Dad?" I called out.

The light disappeared. Sometimes, when a car turned

around in our cul-de-sac, its headlights shone into our house. I listened for the sound of a car motor leaving here, but there was only the distant sound of late-night traffic on El Camino.

Worried, I strained my ears for any further noise from below, but there was only silence. I was just starting to laugh at myself for being so paranoid when I heard the floorboards creak downstairs. I tried to tell myself that it was only the house expanding and contracting. It would be a real joke that of all the houses on Corbenic Court a burglar would pick mine to rob. And then I remembered Russ. Had he come to settle the matter himself?

It was almost as much of a shock as the car crash. It wasn't my feet that stood on the itchy carpet. And it wasn't my eyes that looked out into a house that seemed as dark and frightening as a tomb.

But now was no time to panic. I shook off my fright, telling myself that I was going to move down that hallway just like ... what was it Marsh had said? Yes, a porpoise sliding through a sea of light.

I forced my hand to slide along the hallway wall. I could use that to guide me to Dad's bedroom where there was an extension phone.

Slowly, ever so slowly, like a snail curling itself around a rock, I slid out into the hallway, careful always to keep one hand on the wall to guide me. I tried to remember the distance between Dad's doorway and mine. It was about fifteen feet, I thought. Five steps. That was all. I'd make that easy.

Licking my lips, I shuffled one foot sideways. Then slid the other to join it. So far so good. I slid my left foot out again and then brought my right foot up against it again. Only three more paces to go—I hoped.

The floorboards creaked from near the foot of the stairs, but I told myself to concentrate on the task at hand. It took all of my self-control, but I slid my feet another quiet step.

Suddenly, my groping hand bumped into a metal frame. I'd forgotten all about the picture Dad had hung in the hallway. It was a print made from molded paper pulp with ridges tinted pink and green. It was supposed to be expensive, but it looked to me like someone had just played around with several rolls of toilet paper—only I hadn't said so because Dad was proud of it as an investment. It would be something for my old age, he'd said.

But as it swung back and forth, thumping and scraping against the wall, it didn't seem as if I had much longer to live. Down below, a flashlight snapped on, sending a silvery circle stabbing up the carpeted steps. The circle began to bob as someone started racing heavily up the steps.

I didn't lose any more time as I dashed for Dad's room. Slamming the door shut, I turned the lock on the doorknob. But when they build tract houses, they cut costs. And one of the things they skip is solid doors inside the house. This one was two thin sheets of wood glued and nailed together to form a hollow box. Still, it ought to keep Russ out long enough for me to call the cops.

I hit the light switch with the edge of my hand and saw the telephone on Dad's nightstand beyond the bed. But when I picked up the receiver, I got an odd, buzzing sound. Frantically I dialed the 911 number and then held the receiver up to my ear. No luck. Someone had taken the receiver off the phone downstairs in the kitchen. Since they were both on the same line, I couldn't make a call out.

The footsteps got louder as they came down the hallway toward the room with the lights on. I jumped up from the bed and went to Dad's window, pulling the lever so that the louvered slats opened. "Help, anyone," I shouted at the top of my lungs. "Someone's trying to rob me."

I waited as the cold night air blew into my face. The windows of the neighbors houses remained dark. Either they were asleep or they were ignoring me—if they had even heard me.

The footsteps stopped directly in front of the door. Russ's voice came through the hollow door. "There's no one to help you, Sean."

I was in my pajamas so I didn't have anything that would double as a weapon. Desperately my eyes searched for something I could use to defend myself. "The neighbors know I'm in trouble. The cops will be here any moment."

"I think I'll take my chances. If they do hear you, they'll think it's the TV or just some kind of prank." The doorknob rattled as he tried it. "Everyone assumes that you're safe in your own house.'"

Russ was probably right on that. When I couldn't find a weapon, I tried to bluff Russ by opening a drawer on Dad's nightstand and then slamming it shut. I had some wild notion that maybe I could trick Russ into thinking I'd taken something out. "I've . . . I've got a gun," I said.

"That's strange. Your father said he didn't have one when I asked him that other day." He shook the door impatiently.

"Well, he's going to be back any minute, so you'd better leave." I snatched up a toenail clipper from the top of Dad's bureau; but when I flipped up the top, I found there wasn't any file.

Russ's smugness grated on my nerves. "I thought you'd given up lying, Sean. I know he's down in LA because I arranged for that little computer problem. It's going to keep him busy for quite a few days."

Frantically, I began to search through the clutter on top of the bureau for something with a point—a pair of scissors, a spare set of keys, anything. In the meantime, though, I knew I had to keep Russ talking until I could find something. "Why did you go to all that trouble to get Dad away from here? So you could arrange a little accident for me?"

Russ sounded slightly defensive. "I warned you, remember? But you had to keep prying and snooping. And you even broke into my house. You're nothing but a spoiled little sneak. You were just begging for an 'accident.' So I decided to arrange a little short circuit in your TV."

When I didn't find anything useful on top of the bureau, I began to go through the drawers. "And you figured I'd come bopping home from school, turn on the TV, and zap: one fried Sean."

Russ cleared his throat as if he were embarrassed. "Unh . . . yes. Only you woke up before I could rig the set." His voice took on a hostile note. "I was going to leave, but then I realized that it would suit my purposes almost as well if you died during what appeared to be an ordinary burglary."

The door crashed open. Splinters went flying in the air and the lock itself bent halfway out of the broken door.

Russ was standing there with his right foot still raised in the air. He was in a pair of dark slacks and a dark turtleneck with a ski mask perched on his head. On his hands were a pair of garden gloves, as if he'd had to improvise slightly for his break-in. Around his waist were a number of tools and loops of wire and in his hand was a lit flashlight shining at where the doorknob had been. He stood there for a moment, his radar eyes scanning the room.

His free hand drew a long, thin screwdriver from his belt. Its point was almost as thin and sharp as an ice pick's.

20

IF RUSS THOUGHT HE WAS GOING TO HAVE AN EASY TIME KILLing me, he'd better think again. The door to Dad's bathroom was about five yards behind me. I turned and dashed for it before Russ could stab at me. I think it was out of sheer frustration that he threw the flashlight at me. It thudded against the wall, its glass breaking as the light went out. Then I had shut the door behind me.

But even before I could sigh in relief, Russ was turning the doorknob. For a big man, he could move awfully fast. I hadn't even had a chance to lock it. I threw myself at the door as it began to open. My weight made it move back toward the door frame—but not quite. Russ had managed to wedge his foot into the doorway and he had one hand around the edge of the door.

I didn't give him a chance to use his weight to force his way in: I bit his gloved fingers, closing my jaws hard—harder than I ever had in my life.

Russ howled in pain, and I took a secret joy in it. Russ snatched back his foot and hand. The door slammed shut again and I thumbed the button on the lock.

"Sean," Russ growled, "you know that lock won't keep me out any better than the other one did."

I flipped on the light switch. I had to find a weapon; but there seemed to be even fewer choices in the bathroom than in Dad's bedroom. There was a bar of soap and some towels. I jerked open the medicine cabinet and rummaged around for a razor or even a pack of razor blades. Then I remembered that Dad used an electric shaver now.

I turned around, making a quick survey of the rest of the bathroom. There were a couple of magazines and a pair of soft slippers; and then I caught sight of Dad's hair drier lying on top of the toilet near the sink.

I'd heard about a kid who'd electrocuted himself in the bathtub when he began playing with a hair drier and dropped it into the water. If I could flood the bathroom floor, I could stand on top of the toilet. Then, when Russ tried to break in, he'd step into the water, I could drop the drier into the water and fry him. Actually, I didn't want to kill him—just scare him away.

"Let's not put off the inevitable, shall we?" He rattled the doorknob experimentally.

I reached into the shower stall and aimed the head of the shower toward the door. Twisting both faucets on, I sent a jet of water splashing onto the linoleum floor. Then I put the stopper into the sink and turned on both faucets. While it was filling up, I grabbed Dad's hair drier and plugged it in.

"What are you doing in there?" Russ demanded.

I flicked on the hair drier so that it hummed noisily into life. "Better not come in here," I shouted. "I've got a puddle of water in here and I'll drop this hair drier into it."

"You couldn't have a puddle in there in this short a time," he said suspiciously.

By now the water was splashing noisily over the side of the sink onto the floor, joining the growing pool of water by the shower. But I thought I'd better add to the illusion so I grabbed hold of the plastic cup by the sink, filled it and splashed the water onto the linoleum just beneath the door. Dipping the cup in again I tossed water a second and then a third time at the door.

I tried to sound more confident than I felt. "Well, Russ, why don't you come in. I'd love to see you find out the hard way."

"If you drop the hair drier, you'll die too," Russ warned.

"I found a way that I won't." The hair-drier cord just reached the toilet, and I climbed on top of it.

"You're lying," Russ said, but he didn't sound very positive.

"Maybe. Maybe not." Every second that I delayed Russ meant that my bluff might become a real trap for him.

There was a long silence from the other side of the door. I shut off the hair drier and stepped onto the wet floor. It's surprising how much water you can get in a few minutes. The water already covered the floor of the small bathroom.

I went over to the door and leaned my head against it,

trying to hear Russ. Had I conned him? Had he given up and gone away? Or was he waiting in the bedroom or down the hallway for me to leave my little fort?

I was beginning to know how a mouse felt when it was caught inside one of those wire traps. I'd done a good job of boxing myself into one place. There wasn't any window to climb out of or any weapon I could use to get myself out of here.

I squatted down, trying to fight off a feeling of panic again. There was a cabinet underneath the sink. But the only things in there were some toilet paper, a spray can of bathroom cleaner and one of those little plastic stands with a brush for the toilet bowl.

I looked at the hair drier. Maybe I could strip the wires from the hair drier and wrap them around the doorknob so that Russ would get a nasty surprise when he touched it. That would be a neat trick since he'd originally intended that same fate for me.

I was trying to figure out what I could use to open up the screws of the hair drier when the lights went out.

I stood there in the dark for a moment swearing at the power company. It was a fine time for a blackout. There's somebody at one of the power stations who always knows when you need to cook a special dinner or watch an important football game and turns off your power at that moment.

Then it hit me: Russ could have turned off the circuit breakers that were in the garage. I whipped the useless hair drier away from me and heard it crack against the wall somewhere. I'd wasted all this time trying to rig up a trap when I could have been running over to the neighbor's to call the cops.

I splashed through the water and got to the door. But when I reached for the doorknob, it wasn't there. Or rather, in that pitch blackness, I was trying to find it in the wrong place. Desperately I slid my palm down over the wood grain of the door until my forearm brushed something hard. I grasped the knob in both hands and twisted the button of the lock.

When I opened the door, I found there was some light coming through Dad's windows—whether it was the moon or the street lamps, I wasn't sure. I could make out the nightstand, the bureau and Dad's bed. Like a small kid, I couldn't help wishing that Dad was there. But he wasn't. I was going to have to handle Russ myself.

So think, Sean. Think. If I was in the dark, so was Russ because he'd smashed his flashlight when he threw it at me. That meant he was probably stumbling through our darkened garage unless his eyes really worked like radar. So I had a chance of getting to the front door. But just in case I was wrong, I wanted some kind of weapon.

Suddenly I remembered a TV newscast I'd seen once where the newscasters had been warning parents about the dangers of certain household items, and bathroom cleaner had been on the list. It wasn't a can of mace, but I bet it could hurt if it was sprayed in someone's eyes.

I turned back to the sink. Plunging my hands into the cabinet, I grasped the U-shaped pipe beneath the sink and then the pack of toilet paper. "Come on," I murmured under my breath. "I know you're around there somewhere."

My fingertips slipped over the dusty plastic handle of the toilet-bowl brush. Finally, the back of my hand touched the metal of the can of bathroom cleaner.

The water from the bathroom had made part of the bedroom carpet soggy so that it made squishy noises as I started to run. I may not have been any track star, but I intended to run the fastest fifty-yard obstacle course ever. I sprinted down the hallway, jerking the cap from the can as I did so. I shook it experimentally. It felt awfully light to me.

I could just make out the head of the stairs from the dim light that came from my bedroom window. I didn't even try to slow down when I reached the stairway but let my shoulder hit the wall on the opposite side of the bannister and bounced off it onto the steps.

As I pounded down the stairs, my finger searched for the top of the spray can. There ought to be an arrow marking the direction in which the spray would go. But things that are so easy to do in the light are harder in the dark. I could feel the serrated edges of the arrow but it took me a moment to figure out which way they were pointing.

When I reached the bottom of the stairs, I could see the front door because it was the kind that had panes of glass set in the top half. There wasn't a sign of Russ. Maybe I had the advantage after all since I knew where everything was in the house and he didn't.

I began to laugh with a heady feeling of relief. In just a few seconds I would be outside and yelling my head off. In a minute, I'd have the police. And then all my troubles would be over. People would know just who the real liar was.

I stretched out my left hand because I was holding the can in my right. The doorknob turned okay when I twisted it; but the door itself wouldn't open. "What?" I yanked at the knob again. Russ had locked the dead bolt.

"It's no use," Russ grunted from behind me. I whirled around to find his large silhouette hulking over me. The light from the door panes gleamed wickedly on the screwdriver's tip as he raised it.

"Let's just end this little comedy, shall we?" He started forward.

21

I POINTED THE SPRAY CAN TOWARD WHERE I THOUGHT HIS EYES would be and pressed my finger down hard on the plastic cylinder. I couldn't really see the cloud of spray in the dim light, but the smell stung my nose.

Russ let out a howl. It was like a werewolf cry and an air-raid siren all rolled into one. His head snapped back and he brought his right fist down as he stumbled backward. With a shock I felt a fiery pain slash across my right forearm as his screwdriver cut me. The can almost fell out of my hand, but I managed to hold on.

I brought my left hand to my right forearm. The wound was a slight one, but it was bleeding enough. I could feel the wetness of my own blood. Russ was still yelling as he staggered back a step or two.

There were two other ways out of the house besides the front door. The patio door led into the backyard where I could climb over the neighbor's fence. Or there was the garage which would lead out into the street. But to reach both doors I had to go through the kitchen first. Unfortunately, Russ was between me and either exit. And even though he still couldn't see, he was stabbing at the air with the screwdriver.

The only way left for me to go was back upstairs. Maybe I could get a weapon from Idaho. Dodging around Russ, I raced up the steps, taking them two at a time.

The moon seemed to fill my room with a soft glow so that my bed and shelves and desk stood out as black monstrous heaps. It's strange how night can turn the most familiar things into something else. To buy a little extra time, I wedged my desk chair underneath the doorknob.

Dad had been after me for weeks to clean up my room, so to get him off my back I'd jammed everything into the closet. Now it was filled with a mound of books, magazines, games, shoes and clothes. Buried underneath all that was my baseball bat. It would take forever to dump everything onto the floor.

Russ's heavy footsteps paused at my door. "It's no use hiding, Sean. I'll find you wherever you go." He gave a grunt as he tried the doorknob and found it locked. "Why do you have to keep playing these games?"

Thud.

I nearly jumped when I heard Russ throw himself against the door. I wish I could have seen his face when he realized it wasn't going to break as easily as the other one had.

Thud!

The door seemed to shudder in the frame. I went to my desk to get my scissors. Battles are supposed to happen in Europe and Asia—not in your own bedroom surrounded by all your old, favorite things.

The desk drawers were on the right side. I tugged open the top one and hunted through the broken pencils and junk. If this had been Dad's desk, I would have known exactly where to go because he always kept everything neatly. Of course, my desk was a mess—maybe to prove that I wasn't like him at all. But this was one of the few times when I found myself wishing I had Dad's orderly habits.

THUD.

When I couldn't find anything, I pulled out the second drawer.

THUD! There was the tiniest splintering sound, but the door still held.

When the second drawer proved as full of useless trash as the first, I began a frenzied search through the papers, folders and notebooks piled on top of the desk. Papers went fluttering to the ground. Books and folders and clothing went flying in all directions while my hands groped for the scissors.

THUD! Cr-ra-a-a-ck!

I couldn't help turning around. The upper hinge had broken from the frame so that the top half of my door was tilting inward, leaving a space between the door and the frame itself. But the chair was still holding the door up. Russ's face appeared in the space. "There's no way out now."

I raised the spray can. "If you come any closer, I'll use this again." I took a step toward him, hoping that I could keep him from pulling the chair away from the doorknob.

"Not this time, Sean." His right hand suddenly appeared above his head. He'd replaced his screwdriver with a long, wicked-looking knife from our kitchen. He held it ready to slash at me if I tried to get near him as his left hand groped for the chair beneath the doorknob.

My stomach felt as if someone were drawing it into a tight knot. I pivoted to begin searching for the scissors when I saw the window again. If I could get through it and onto our slanting roof, I could probably keep Russ from getting up there. At least the odds were better than if I stayed here.

The only problem was the louvered glass. Why couldn't the builders have put in regular windows? I'd have to smash the glass slats to get outside.

I dropped the spray can with a hollow clink and snatched up my desk lamp, yanking the plug free from the wall outlet. I swung the lamp over my head and brought it down against the glass slats. They cracked but they didn't break. So I swung my lamp again, but this time with all my strength. They broke this time, making a sound like a thousand crystal bells shattering.

Behind me, I could hear the chair crash away from the door. The wind blew in through the broken window and with it came the promise of freedom. There were still jagged pieces of glass in the metal slots of the window frame, but most of the glass had fallen outside with the lamp. The few shards on the rug were too puny to be useful against Russ's knife. I glanced over my shoulder to see Russ's hand on the button of the doorknob. He'd be in the room in a moment.

Careful to avoid the glass, I put my hands on the sides and I pulled myself up so that I was standing on the window sill. I leaned out, stretching my right arm to reach the gutter. Its metal sides felt awfully thin and soft. But if Dad had done his usually thorough job, I knew he would have hammered in enough nails to keep a hurricane from blowing it away. It ought to take my weight long enough for me to swing myself onto the roof. I caught a glimpse of the driveway from the corner of my eye. It was only twenty feet to the ground but it seemed so much farther. Cautiously I extended my left arm beyond my right and moved my right hand further along the gutter. In a moment, I could pull myself up onto the roof, beyond Russ's reach.

22

I TURNED AROUND TO FACE THE HOUSE SO I COULD LOOK AT where I was climbing. Russ was almost on top of me. I twisted to my right just in time. Russ lunged through the window, his knife thrusting at the air instead of into my heart.

He looked surprised. His head turned slightly and he started to bring his knife around in a backhanded slash. But I was just a little quicker. Twisting slightly, I closed my legs around Russ's waist. Using a scissors hold, I pulled him off his feet so that most of his body was outside the window sill.

The edges of the rain gutter cut painfully into my fingers and the whole thing began to creak dangerously as it tried to support our combined weights.

"Help me back inside," Russ said in a tight, strangled voice.

Maybe it was the adrenaline or maybe I just didn't care anymore. "Why should I?" I laughed.

The gutter gave a groan as it loosened from the wall.

"Because we'll both die otherwise." Russ's voice came out high and shrill. "Look, I'll tell the police everything. Everything."

"Liar," I said, and took a savage delight in calling him that.

His left arm tightened around my legs. "If I fall, so will you."

I tightened my legs around him right away, like I wanted to cut him in two, and dragged him toward the glass shards on one side of the window. I felt some of the glass stab me in the side of the leg at the same time Russ gave a yelp of pain. I doubt if our wounds were more than slight cuts; but it surprised Russ enough so that he let go.

"No, no," he screamed. The knife dropped from his hand and he tried to stretch his hands behind him to grab hold of my legs again; but they were already beyond his reach.

But before I could say or do anything, the rain gutter gave one last moan and a whole section broke off in my hands. I had just one moment to brace my foot against the wall and try to kick myself toward the side where the big, sprawling bottle bush was. A moment later, I was dropping through the air.

Beneath me, Russ was falling with his arms spread, like a huge dark bird with skinny wings. The boards of the house zipped by and yet my eyes seemed to snap precise pictures so that little details wore clear in my mind—how the sides of the boards were edged in shadow, how the brushes had created small swirls of paint on the boards.

There was a sickening thud as Russ hit the driveway; and I wondered if that was going to happen to me too. So I could have shouted for joy the next moment when I crashed into the prickly bottle bush. The top branches hit my back hard like the thongs of a whip; but none of them was strong enough to stop my fall. The leaves fluttered all around me like so many dark moths, and suddenly I came up hard against the fork of two larger branches.

I hit with enough force at the base of my back to drive the breath from me; but at least it had slowed down my fall. The gutter clattered onto the driveway before I tumbled backwards out of the bush onto the concrete.

As far as I was concerned that bush was never going to get a trim.

I lay there for a moment, wondering if I had broken something. After all, you read about people who are paralyzed for life from tripping on a step, let alone tumbling out of a second-story window. I swung my arms out experimentally and felt the leaves of the bottle bush tickle my left hand with cool, feathery touches. Worried, I tried to move my legs and found I could bend them too. Reassured, I took a deep breath of the night air and savored the wonderful moist smell of our lawn. The entire world seemed so fresh and crisp that I felt like a whole new person too.

The lights went on in the Weisses' house. I guess Russ's scream had woken them up finally. And I found myself looking up at a sleepy Nora standing in her window as she finished tying her bathrobe around her. I tried to tell her to call the cops, but the words came out as a croak.

And then Russ whimpered. "Please, God, no, not this."

I sat up with great care. Russ lay in a dark heap on the driveway. The fallen, twisted section of the gutter seemed to point between him and me. I got up shakily. The knife lay about a foot from his head. I edged in and knocked it away with the side of my foot.

Russ rolled his eyes so he could look at me from the corners. His voice rose fearfully. "I can't turn my head."

I approached him cautiously, but he didn't snatch at me. He just lay there on his back.

He was panicked. "I can't move my legs or my arms."

I stared down into Russ's eyes as he began to realize the truth: the fall had paralyzed him. And I hope I never see a look like that again. His eyes were open wide and seemed mostly white. And it was like Russ was still falling—falling into a bottomless pit. This was one punishment for which all his money and lawyers were useless.

I shivered. In some ways, it would have been kinder to him if he had died from the fall.

And the hatred just drained out of me like the water in a sink when you pull out a stopper. I think Marsh would have said this was enough.

Russ's face contorted in fear. "Help me, Sean," he whispered. "Help me."

I almost felt sorry for him. "I'll get an ambulance."

"No, don't leave," he begged.

And I remembered how I had stood here just the other night, thinking about how terrible it was to be alone in the cold and dark. And Russ was more isolated than even I had been because he was lost now somewhere in that body of his. He wasn't a monster now, he was just one more lonely, frightened human being.

"Okay," I said.

And then the door to the Weisses' house had opened and Nora was running out toward me.

ABOUT THE AUTHOR

LAURENCE YEP IS THE AUTHOR OF THREE NOVELS ABOUT Chinese-Americans: *Dragonwings,* which was a 1976 Newbery Honor Book; *Child of the Owl,* winner of the 1977 Boston Globe-Horn Book Fiction Award; and *Sea Glass.* He is also the author of three science fiction novels: *Sweetwater, Sea Demons,* and *Dragon of the Lost Sea* (an ALA Notable Book).

Mr. Yep grew up in San Francisco, where he was born. He now lives in Sunnyvale, California.